LESSONS IN

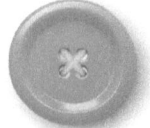 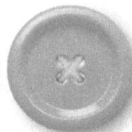    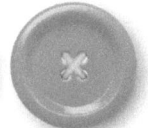

PHILANTHROPY

     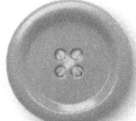

   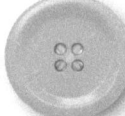  

The Legacy of **Barb McInnes**

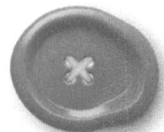     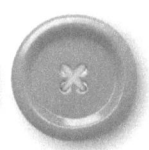

AS SHARED WITH GLENN McINNES

GROWING COMMUNITY FOUNDATIONS TO BUILD COMMUNITIES

Like the buttons on our clothes,
philanthropy holds our world together.

And yet buttons, like charitable giving,
often go unnoticed.

Lessons in Philanthropy provides insights on how the work of
Barb McInnes, in her 25 years at the Ottawa Community Foundation,
built an enduring approach to giving and community.

The Ottawa Community Foundation's story began in 1986
and achieved $1 million in grants in six years.

In 2024, the Foundation had assets of $281 million and
granted $50 million to 872 charities.

Lessons in Philanthropy—The Legacy of Barb McInnes
Copyright © 2025 Glenn McInnes
Published by Piccadilly Press
ISBN 978-0-920736-02-9

All rights reserved. No part of this publication may be reproduced, stored in any material form (including photocopying or storing it in any medium by electronic means and whether or not transiently or incidentally to some other use of this publication) without the written permission of the copyright holder except in accordance with the provisions of the Copyright Act. Applications for the copyright holder's written permission to reproduce any part of this publication should be addressed to the publisher.

Warning: The doing of an unauthorized act in relation to a copyrighted work may result in both a civil claim for damages and criminal prosecution.

IMPORTANT: The opinions expressed herein are solely those of the authors. To ensure the currency of the information presented, readers are strongly encouraged to solicit the assistance of appropriate professionals.

Piccadilly Press
514 Piccadilly Ave.
Ottawa ON
K1Y 0H8
McInnes@BarbarasLegacy.ca

BarbarasLegacy.ca

Edited by: Lisa MacDonald
Design by: John VanDuzer, *Wishart by Banko Creative Studio*

To Barb,
Leah and Emily,
and our grandchildren,
Devon, Simon and Gideon.

TESTIMONIALS

We Americans have a lot to learn

"This book about the work of an extraordinary individual is an antidote to the arrogance of power that can plague, not just organized philanthropy, but our nation states as well. We Americans have a lot to learn from our Canadian neighbors about how big money cannot solve problems in isolation from a community's (or nation's) multiple constituencies. Through the testimonials of real people in the field, this book brings to life the basic principles of effective philanthropy. We may think we already know the lessons—but we are more likely to put them into practice after reading the thoughtful, candid and inspiring examples before us."

Char Mollison
Vice President (retired), Council on Foundations
Past Chair, CAF America
Senior Fellow, Center on Nonprofits, Philanthropy and Social Enterprise
George Mason University USA

"A rare and true glimpse into the challenges, decisions, and quiet triumphs that define community leadership. These stories will resonate with leaders of community foundations, past and present, as they speak to the beauty and complexity of building trust, shifting power, and navigating relationships across sectors and communities—and how Barb did it all with grace and determination."

Andrea Dicks
President
Community Foundations of Canada

"This book is a meaningful legacy for change-makers in the community foundations movement across the world. At this time, when humanity seems to be lacking social imagination to "think big" in the face of today's challenges of inequalities, threats to democracy and climate change, Barbara's legacy is immensely precious."

Carola Carazzone
Segretaria generale
Assifero—Associazione italiana delle fondazioni ed enti filantropici, Roma
Vice-President
Philea—Philanthropy Europe Association

"At a time of overwhelming gloom about the dismal state of the world, Barb's legacy remains highly relevant to all of us: with perseverance, humour, joy and love, what initially seems impossible becomes possible when building inclusive and dynamic communities."

Jean-Marc Mangin
President & CEO
Philanthropic Foundations Canada

A treasure trove of ideas

"Barbara McInnes was a bold, visionary thinker who could turn big ideas into action. She was also an inspirational teacher whose regular guest lectures in the Master of Philanthropy and Nonprofit Leadership (MPNL) at Carleton University were greatly valued by both students and faculty. Barb continues teaching us through the contributions of this book. It offers important lessons for leadership in building stronger, more vibrant communities, and is a must read for anyone seeking to make a difference through philanthropy. For those working in, or with, community foundations across Canada and internationally, this book is a treasure trove of ideas for nurturing authentic relationships and trust with boards, donors, grantees and community organizations."

Susan Phillips
Professor Emerita
Philanthropy and Nonprofit Leadership
School of Public Policy and Administration
Carleton University

"Mahatma Ghandi's quote, "be the change that you wish to see in the world" captures Barb's wisdom. Change comes from within, a lesson that is often lost in our world today. Barb shared a story of a family trip she made to Kerala, India. Barb described being welcomed and invited to join the community in celebrating festivals and events. In a place where Barb could have felt a lack of belonging due to cultural and language barriers, she was right at home. Her smile, love of people and authentic curiosity in others allowed her sense of belonging to flourish. Barb's essence removed the barriers that would normally inhibit human connection. This was a real-life example of being the change you wish to see in the world."

Andrew Chunilall CPA, CA, ICD.D, ACC
Past Chair, Wings (Worldwide Initiatives for Grantmaker Support)
Chair, Forward Global Canada
CEO, Community Foundations of Canada

A little bit of mischief

"Barb McInnes was an inspired and inspiring leader with much to teach all community foundations and funds. Her principles of leading with humility, curiosity, passion and a little bit of mischief have vaulted the Ottawa Community Foundation to great success and secured her position as a significant influence in community foundations across Canada as well as internationally. The lessons her friends and colleagues recount in this book can be applied broadly to both start-ups or well-established funds and are valuable tools for establishing their principles and approach."

Edith Cody-Rice
Committee Member and Donor
Mississippi Mills Community Fund

"This book is a warm and honest tribute to Barb McInnes, who led with love for her community and helped shape what community foundations have become today. Barb understood that local action is powerful, but she also saw the value of connecting that work nationally and internationally. She supported the first steps of community foundations in Eastern Europe and helped open doors for the model to grow in large parts of Europe—including Germany—where her approach to donor-advised funds left a lasting impression.

What stood out about Barb wasn't just her leadership, but how she made people feel. She listened, she trusted, and she encouraged at a time when the idea of community foundations was still new in many European countries. This book reflects that spirit."

Dr. Kathrin Dombrowski
Coordinating Director
European Community Foundation Initiative (ECFI)

Raise expectations, not just funds

"I see *Lessons in Philanthropy: The Legacy of Barb McInnes* as both an inspiration and a guide for those in small Association of Fundraising Professionals' chapters or nonprofit organizations. It offers a compelling model of leadership grounded in humility, vision, and heart. Barb's story reminds us that even a small platform can create lasting impact. Barb didn't just raise funds—she raised expectations."

Christina Morgan, CFRE
Past President
AFP Newfoundland and Labrador

"The insights that Barbara imparted to those she collaborated with, resonate throughout the stories in this book. I am reminded of how essential good governance is—necessitating robust leadership, the establishment of diverse boards, and the cultivation of a learning culture during uncertain times. As a master connector, Barbara and I envisioned the creation of environments where individuals would feel a sense of belonging."

Roger D. Ali
Social Sector Executive & Consultant
AFP Global Board Chair

TABLE OF CONTENTS

Acknowledgements 1
Foreword 3
Preface 5
Introduction 7

Philanthropy 11
1 Plant an Acorn 13
2 Operation Come Home 15
3 Leveraging and Multiplying Good 17
4 Youth Directing Philanthropy 19
5 Turning Good Ideas into Reality 21
6 Becoming a Learning Organization 23
7 "Think Big" 26
8 You Don't Have to be a Millionaire to Make a Difference 29

Leadership 31
9 Teaching and Leading 33
10 Aligning Values to Action 36
11 A Love for Humanity 38
12 Ask, Don't Tell 41
13 Illumination as an Approach to Learning 43
14 Investing in People 45
15 A Mentor and a Coach 48
16 Three Lessons in Leadership 50

Community 53
17 Serenity Renewal for Families 55
18 Rideau Street Youth 58
19 The OCRI School Breakfast Program 60

20 The Founding of PAL Ottawa 62
21 A Vision of Community... 64
22 A How-To in Community Building—Kindness as a Constant 66

Ottawa Community Foundation 69
23 A Primer on Community Funding 71
24 In Support of Visual Arts Organizations 74
25 City of Ottawa Poverty Reduction Committee 76
26 It Began with The Nominating Committee 78
27 The Growth of the Ottawa Community Foundation 80
28 Thirteen Years of Service on the OCF Board 83
29 From Intern to Staff at OCF 86

Beyond Borders 89
30 Building Community in Eastern Europe 91
31 West-Vlaanderen Community Foundation 95
32 Community Foundations of Canada 97
33 Massawippi Foundation—No Giving Up 100
34 The Community Foundation of Hanover 102
35 Building Communities Nationally and Internationally 104
36 Community Foundation for Ireland 107

Contributor Bios 109
Barbara McInnes, C.M. (1943-2021) 123

Appendix | Lessons in Philanthropy—Summary 127
Appendix | Growing the Ottawa Community Foundation 131
Appendix | Growth Cycles of Community Foundations 135

ACKNOWLEDGEMENTS

This book would not have been published without the unwavering support and advice of Russ Mills and Jackie Holzman. Russ attended every meeting and most of the interviews, and Jackie kept us focused on what we had to do next. Russ and Jackie witnessed and participated in Barb's philanthropic work as friends and colleagues for more than a quarter of a century.

The first person I spoke to about this book was Eric Fletcher. Eric worked for me when he was a student in computer science at the University of Waterloo. Eric is the smartest high-tech person I've ever known, and among his many accomplishments, is publishing 300+ online books. Eric helped me understand how a book is published and gave me the best advice a beginner could possibly have: "Get an editor right from the beginning, and make sure it's not your aunt."

I do have the best Editor—Lisa MacDonald—an accomplished non-fiction book editor specializing in philanthropy. She is also the Editor-in-Chief of Hilborn Charity eNEWS and Foundation Magazine. She has helped many writers successfully bring their books to market. Her guidance was key to moving this project through to completion, including bringing a creative and visionary book designer on board, John VanDuzer.

Our Online Publishing Lead, Kailey Oliver is a successful self-published author and social marketing professional. She wrote "Paint Your Universe: Inspirational Poetry" and "World Stained Us, System Blamed Us." Chris Jones, the former webmaster at the Ottawa Citizen and co-founder of Management Vitality Inc., also contributed his exceptional skills and knowledge of self-publishing.

Brent Eades is the best website architect I could ever hope for, who in retirement has generously helped hundreds of nonprofits. A former Communications

Advisor with the Bank of Canada, Brent served on the Board of Directors and was an Online Advisor to the Michener Awards Foundation and is the Editor-in-Chief of The Millstone News.

Jenn Campbell helped convert all the audio interviews to text. Anne Carlysle told me that every story needs a takeaway. Edith Cody-Rice pointed out that every community foundation start-up (including hers) could learn from this book. Ken Hoffman helped me focus on philanthropy recipients. Grant Jameson has been so supportive of Barb. Thank you to Pam Martin, Barb's best friend in high school, for her insights and to Marcia McClung, whose grandmother Nellie was Barb's grandmother's friend and neighbour in Edmonton. Nicole Milne helped put the book back in gear. Jocelyn Patton shared how to be successful at self-publishing. Caroline Phillips told me she has more photos of Barb than anyone, and that I could use any of them. Peter Simpson and Penny Williams provided me with sound advice.

A huge thank you to the thirty-six contributors to this book, including Zita Cobb, who told me that a poem is a distilled-down story, in which case Zita must (most of all) be a poet.

And finally, **Lessons in Philanthropy** wouldn't have been possible without my closest advisors on philanthropy and on their mother—Leah McInnes Eustace, ACFRE and Emily McInnes.

— **Glenn McInnes**

FOREWORD

We live in a terrible world.
We live in a wonderful world.
The world will be what we make it.
   – Kate Marvel, climate author, NASA

Barb McInnes showed us how to make the world. Lucky us who knew her and learned directly from her.

These lessons in philanthropy, from the legacy of Barb McInnes, are a primer on "how to be" and how to get good things done in this world we are making.

The stories are testimonials to the rare force of energy, joy, patience, clarity and light that was Barb McInnes. They also show us how to see the world underneath the world, how to see the potential that exists just beyond what is readily visible and how to call, nudge and encourage people to their best. Barb knew that courage comes from encouragement—these stories show us how to encourage.

If you missed the opportunity to work with Barb, then this book is for you. It knits together learnings from Barb in thirty-six accessible, relatable, doable lessons.

If you knew Barb, this book is for you, too. As she did in life, Barb continues to draw us together. We need that now more than ever. The challenges facing us are not simple and we desperately need the sum of our actions to add up. This book holds insights for aligning energies, for seeing the connective tissue and, most of all, for activating the "us" in everything.

Thank you, Barb, and thank you Glenn for bringing the lessons in this book to life.

— **Zita Cobb**

PREFACE

When I first joined the Ottawa Community Foundation, one name came up over and over again: Barbara McInnes. People didn't just talk about her as a former CEO. They talked about her as the heart of the Foundation. They talked about her as a connector, builder and champion. Over time, as I found my feet in my new role at the Foundation, I came to understand exactly why.

Barb didn't set out to build an institution.

She set out to build a community where generosity wasn't something abstract, it was personal—rooted in relationships. It was about helping Ottawa become a place where everyone could thrive. She understood that the strength of a community foundation is not in its balance sheet, but in the trust that is built, the conversations that it sparks, and the steady work of bringing people together to make something good happen.

Barb made a lot of good things happen.

Under her leadership, the Foundation grew from modest beginnings into a respected and trusted part of Ottawa's civic fabric but, it wasn't just the growth of the endowment or the grants that defined Barb's leadership. It was the way she led—with warmth and curiosity, and always with an open door and open heart. She believed that everyone had something to offer—whether it was a new idea, a major gift or simply a willingness to listen and learn.

Barb was a builder of bridges.

She brought together donors and community leaders; charities and business people; policymakers and neighbours. She saw connections where others saw gaps and she understood that the Foundation could be more than a place where people gave—it could be a place where people gathered, dreamed, and acted together.

Even today, many years after her official retirement, I see Barb's fingerprints on all our work. I see it in the way we show up in community conversations, in the way we treat our donors as partners, and in the way we always ask ourselves not just "what can we do?" but "what more is possible?"

It's a rare thing to leave behind an organization stronger than you found it. It's even rarer to leave behind a spirit and a culture that continues to inspire everyone who walks through the doors. That is Barb's gift to the Foundation, and to all of us who have the privilege of carrying her work forward.

This book is a tribute to Barb's leadership, her legacy and the countless ways that she shaped— not just the Ottawa Community Foundation—but the city itself.

Thank you, Barb. Ottawa is better because of you.

Michael Maidment
President & CEO
Ottawa Community Foundation

INTRODUCTION

In many respects, *Lessons in Philanthropy: The Legacy of Barb McInnes* is a love letter to Barb, written by those who worked with her, those who were supported by the Ottawa Community Foundation (OCF) and those who were inspired by Barb's example as a community leader. However, Barb was a humble person who didn't talk about her insights into philanthropy or life. In this book, thirty-six people have shared *their* stories—documenting journeys they took with Barb or the OCF.

Barbara worked tirelessly to enhance philanthropy in Ottawa for almost four decades. She built community with exceptional dedication. She brought energy and excitement, balanced with wisdom and intelligence to every endeavour, always with good humour and a generosity of spirit. Barbara was a force for good. She developed new avenues and partnerships that enabled generous citizens to invest in their community and so the legacy that she built lives on.

This book is a witness to its time but even more enduring, is the footprint of Barbara's work at the Ottawa Community Foundation and the "lessons" that endure for upcoming leaders.

Barb consummately cared about other people. She approached her relationships with a singular focus and each person always received her full attention. She had a great curiosity about people and places, and advocating for philanthropy was second nature for her.

At the same time, Barb held an overarching view of the impact that charities, donors and the foundation had on the communities that they serve. It is my sincere hope that this book will carry this view forward.

Barb cared deeply about her community and the people who make up that community. The thirty-six stories in this book describe some of Barb's achievements during her stewardship. I believe she was mindful that she was building a movement that would continue to grow and increase its impact in the community.

Between 1988 and 2013, philanthropy saw significant shifts. This included an increase in wealthy individuals donating to charitable causes and a broadening of philanthropic areas to include arts and culture and the environment, with community foundations taking an active role in social change.

Barb was at the forefront of a transformation in philanthropy that the stories in this book chronicle.

Private giving from individuals experienced substantial growth, often spurred by increased economic prosperity. Foundations began to explore social enterprises and innovative solutions to social problems and foundations became engaged internationally, addressing global changes like more social societies.

My love, friendship and camaraderie with Barb evolved over 63 years, starting when we were only 16 years of age. The stories of impact shared by the authors of this book, often had a similar evolution, over 30 years. If this is your first time meeting Barb, I hope you will feel inspired by her dedication, gratitude and commitment to the people and projects that she felt so fortunate to be a part of.

Barb and I enjoyed our life every day and constantly said how lucky we were to have the family and friends that we had, and to have the privilege to visit the places we travelled to.

In 2008, Barb was awarded the Order of Canada and in 2021, Barb became the first recipient of the AFP Ottawa Chapter Lifetime Achievement Award in recognition of her many extraordinary contributions as a community champion. AFP also announced a new program in Barbara's honour, The Barbara McInnes Executive Mentoring Project Fund to nurture leadership capacity and mentorship in Ottawa's nonprofit sector.

On July 1, 2021, Barbara passed away in the arms of her family in her home in Ottawa.

This book is a tribute to the lifetime dedication and commitment of Barbara, and everyone who builds communities together.

Lessons in Philanthropy: The Legacy of Barb McInnes is supplemented by a website *BarbarasLegacy.ca*. We invite you to visit this site to share your personal experiences with philanthropy and the lessons presented through the sharing of these stories.

Glenn McInnes
Ottawa, ON Canada
June, 2025

PHILANTHROPY

"Our growing success in partnering and forging relationships with other philanthropic groups, different levels of government and corporations is important.

It means the Community Foundation is playing a key role in the center of philanthropy in the city— a role we have earned through the strong credibility we've established."

Barbara McInnes

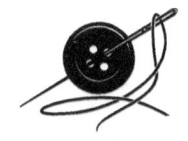

Plant an Acorn
Jackie Holzman

LESSON 1
We build community for the future and we don't do it alone.

It is said that there are three distinctive philanthropic traditions: relief, improvement and social reform.

This was Barbara McInnes' mantra.

First, stop the bleeding. Then, determine the cause. Finally, prevent it from happening again.

Barb convinced the city to transfer funds in the Ottawa Foundation to launch the new Community Foundation of Ottawa-Carleton. Its logo represented this philanthropic idea; if you want a forest then plant an acorn, a tree will grow and someone else will enjoy the shade.

As a former politician, I know too often we are only thinking of the "now." Barb reminded me that we build our community for the future and we don't do it alone. Each individual is a building block and all are required in the construction.

Barb was a mentor. She was a role model.

Be inclusive.

Be transparent.

Give people agency.

Build collaboration.

And, always say thank you!

Our nation's capital Ottawa, Canada and the world of philanthropy are better because of all the acorns Barb planted.

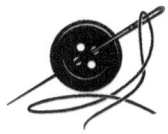

Operation Come Home
Elspeth McKay

LESSON 2
Small grassroots organizations can have a lot of impact for a small amount of money.

Barb was a colleague and friend when I worked at Causeway and afterwards when I became Executive Director of Operation Come Home (OCH). OCH's finances were precarious in 2007, and Barb was one of the only funders with a good understanding of what OCH was trying to accomplish.

In 2007, OCH was operating a non-traditional, one-room classroom (with a seconded high school teacher in partnership with the Catholic school board) as well as a drop-in. Barb and the community foundation played a critical role as our budget grew from $465,000 to $2.8 million over 15 years. She had an uncanny way of understanding exactly what very small grassroots organizations were trying to do. She knew we could have a lot of impact for a very small amount of money and would ensure that we received annual funding for various programs and social enterprises and encouraged our social entrepreneurial spirit.

And not just us.

Barb would convene meetings with nonprofit groups to forge a common goal. She would come up with a solution with all the parties at the table, each one assigned a role unique to their asset or expertise. This was unusual. Many social service sector organizations are forced to compete for funding, and typically don't want to partner with other organizations. As a funder, Barb understood this. She was not the funder we were used to.

Barb would let us do the work, without a lot of evaluation and reporting required by government. She was always present at our annual general meetings and face-to-face meetings and she was very interested in the young people we served, who primarily came out of the child welfare system. She shared our view that we had to lift people up by providing resources and supports required for employment, so the homeless would find jobs and not go in and out of the system—commonly known as the revolving door syndrome. Over time, the community foundation provided funds that would positively impact many young people who became employed and housed. They no longer had to rely on community housing and welfare.

Barb was unique—running a foundation with creativity and an understanding of the importance of small grassroots organizations. Were it not for her, many small organizations probably would not have survived. OCH relied heavily on Barb and the foundation to provide funds to keep us going and to make sure that there was a place for young people to go. Now, we have a lot of supporters, donors and stakeholders. People tell us, "…you helped my brother, or my sister reunite with the family", or "I was a parent of someone that you reunited", or "my son got a job/ finished high school/ is now in university because of one of your programs." Barb and the community foundation helped us change lives and save lives.

There are very few executives in a funding position who can identify with smaller organizations that need funding, yet come with more risks in comparison to larger government-funded entities.

Large funders and nonprofits tend to be risk adverse, while smaller nonprofits are "on the ground" doing the work instead of branding their organization or doing marketing and fundraisers. Barbara respected that. She wasn't interested in press conferences or recognition plaques. She wanted the money to go directly to serving young people and getting the results we wanted to deliver. Barb accepted the organization's view of what money was needed and how they would use it and she didn't nickel and dime every expense line.

Barb was a creative out-of-the-box thinker with an interest in organizations and people who also demonstrated unique and innovative ideas and ways of thinking.

Leveraging and Multiplying Good
Russ Mills

LESSON 3
Skillful management of one donor's generosity can lead to greater impact and a pipeline of support.

In 1998, Urbandale Construction, one of Ottawa's largest home builders, was planning to celebrate their 40th year in business. The two founders of the company, Herb Nadolny and Lyon Sachs, invited me to a meeting at their head office to outline their plans. I was publisher of the Ottawa Citizen at the time and knew them as large advertisers.

Herb and Lyon told me that they had a budget of $400,000 to celebrate the 40th anniversary, but instead of spending it on promotion and parties for the company they wanted to put the money back into the community and try to do as much good as possible. This would be their way of thanking the community for being the source of their success as builders. They asked for the Citizen's help in donating this money in the best possible way.

I told them that the Citizen would be happy to help, but that I would also like to involve the Community Foundation of Ottawa which had expertise in local philanthropy. I had recently joined the Board of Governors of the Foundation and had been impressed with its operations.

I approached Barbara McInnes, CEO of the Foundation, told her of Urbandale's plans and asked for her help in giving away the money in the most effective way. Barb leapt at the opportunity in her typical helpful and enthusiastic manner. She determined the greatest needs for the money and, by using the Urbandale donations to lever matching funds from government programs and other donors, was able to turn the $400,000 from Urbandale into a significantly larger amount.

The money helped hungry children, seniors, community recreation and housing programs. The owners of Urbandale were delighted with the good their donations had accomplished. The company was so pleased that they did it again with $500,000 for their 50th anniversary and $600,000 for their 60th year in business.

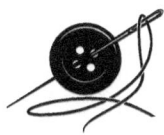

Youth Directing Philanthropy
Medin Admasu

LESSON 4
How you approach a situation will dictate how you come up with solutions and outcomes.

I met Barb in 2004 while attending university. She interviewed me to be an advisor for a newly launched youth philanthropy program at the Ottawa Community Foundation (OCF).

Barb and I didn't know each other but she was very open and easy to talk to. My job was to help recruit 14 to 18-year-olds to an organization that had never dealt with young people, and make sure they felt comfortable. The youth that signed up for this type of opportunity tended to be more comfortable in youth centers, rather than offices. The OCF was a different kind of space with high-net-worth donors. It felt like a "corporate" nonprofit world.

If youth are not comfortable, they're not going to show up. We had to involve the new recruits, anticipating their questions about the program. A grant-making committee for young people was formed. Making granting decisions was empowering; a big responsibility for teenagers but Barb made sure they knew that they could be open and honest.

For most, it was their first experience on a youth council or in a youth group. They learned the basics: to have a meeting agenda, to show up on time and to follow up on items after the meeting. We had access to various people at the foundation, including board members. The program committee chair, Manjit

Basi, took a special interest in our committee and was always available for questions.

All the youth that participated in the program enjoyed themselves, and have done well for themselves in school and/or career. One of the student Chairs is now a surgeon and another works for a large pension plan. It wasn't a big committee—only 15 or 16 young people.

At the time this program began, there were very few groups involving youth in decision-making in philanthropy. We had $30,000 in funds available, usually granting out $10,000 in each round. It felt like a big deal for youths to give $500 or $1,000 grants to other youth groups!

A lot of our youth participants came from my personal connections. I grew up in social housing, so I knew a lot of people from those neighborhoods. I recruited from my networks, and the groups I had been part of, including my family's background in the Ethiopian community.

Barb had confidence we could figure it out. The Community Foundation wanted to engage youth and didn't know how best to do it. Their approach wasn't prescriptive. Barb would say, "This is what we're thinking. Can you figure out how to do it?"

Today, I'm the Program Manager at the Boys and Girls Club serving almost 5000 kids every year with a budget of over $8 million. My experience with the Ottawa Community Foundation, as facilitated by Barbara McInnes taught me about making grants. I was around social workers my whole life and grew up going to the Boys and Girls Club and youth centres.

I've been involved in the sector since I was 14 and I'm 40 now.

I learned from Barb's example. She was always enthusiastic with a big smile. She was not just personable; Barb created a positive and uplifting atmosphere whenever she entered a room. Her approach was consistent, whether at meetings or events. I realized early on that this was the way to build relationships with people. You create the space that you want people to excel in.

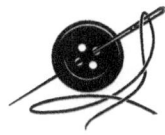

Turning Good Ideas into Reality
Wendy Muckle

LESSON 5
Taking a leap of faith and supporting a "wild" idea can have long-term positive outcomes.

When you are trying to do things that have never been done before, it's usually very difficult to convince funders to take the leap of faith and support your "wild" idea.

Barbara, and by association the Ottawa Community Foundation, was always someone who was not afraid to invest in an idea even if it meant helping you get the knowledge needed to make it work. I started to work directly with Barb in 2001 when Ottawa Inner City Health (OICH) was starting. We were full of good ideas but no resources to make them a reality.

Most people don't know that many of the successful innovations in harm reduction in Ottawa started with small amounts of funding from the Community Foundation supported very personally by Barbara McInnes. Barb really cared about the people who were struggling the most and she did not back off from supporting ideas to help them which were unproven and controversial. She really saw the value of doing the right thing and not necessarily what convention viewed as acceptable at the time.

Barbara was the one who fought hard for funding the two-year pilot project which generated the Managed Alcohol programs of today. From a six-person pilot project, Managed Alcohol has grown into an international best practice intervention supported from a national community of practice and research operating in almost every major city in Canada. Not a bad return on investment!

Ottawa Inner City Health's approach to improving health literacy among the homeless is entirely due to the support of the Community Foundation and a project which Barbara was strongly invested in. When efforts to improve life expectancy among the homeless started to succeed, Inner City Health faced a new challenge of helping people learn to live well with chronic health conditions. Improving health literacy among people with very low literacy levels, high rates of cognitive impairments and a history of poor academic experiences was no simple task when all conventional approaches failed. To go to anyone but Barbara to ask for money to translate chronic disease management information into a delivery format based on the strengths of street culture would have been a very hard sell but it was an idea that captivated her imagination. It is also a program which was so successful, that it is still offered in all OICH supportive housing programs.

Whether it was harm reduction, palliative care or helping Inuit people explain things in their own voice, Barbara very much believed—not only in helping those who needed it most—but in their right to do so on their own terms and in their own way. This belief underpinned much of her work at the Ottawa Community Foundation and is imprinted in the corporate culture to this day.

Becoming a Learning Organization
Vinod Rajasekaran

> **LESSON 6**
> Having a forward-looking mindset sets the stage for collaboration, innovation and change.

I'd heard stories about Barb's generosity, thoughtfulness and kindness and her sense of humour. Ian Bird, who ran Community Foundations of Canada (CFC), had told me about his vision to bring more innovation and creativity to CFC and was fascinated by what we wanted to do at Impact Hub Ottawa and said "there's one-person I'm going to bring to your opening that you should meet—Barb McInnes." Our opening was an incredible day and a terrible day. The Hub was on the sixth floor, and we had one small elevator which broke down that morning and we couldn't get it fixed.

Barb was the first to make it up the six flights, without Ian. But Barb was much older than Ian and Ian is a two-time Olympian, right? But there's Ian behind her, totally out of breath. She's smiling and full of energy as she walks in. In 45 seconds, I'd made up my mind. There was a sense of thoughtfulness and openness about her that was very rare.

Barb and I talked about her vision for the city and the work she was doing. She was very curious. "Who are all these people? Tell me about the hub network, where did it start?" And that's how Barb began to contribute to our journey at the Hub. We met and talked regularly about social finance and social enterprise, and social innovation and nonprofits, and foundations, and what could be done to improve the city.

Barb knew deep down that all kinds of people and organizations needed to come together. She saw how the Hub brought people together in a community. She also had a deep desire to contribute to our types of initiatives. This was a profound experience for me. It showed there were people that thought differently, and had a forward-looking mindset about how change happens when people come together, and how collaboration and an exchange of ideas can happen to create new initiatives. I had this idea that CEOs of big organizations had a lot of ego and big personalities, but Barb debunked that.

There is one thing that Barb really catalyzed, and we accomplished together for the Hub. I asked Barb, what's holding nonprofits and charities back? Is it people? Is it funding? Is it talent? She said, "People don't want to fail. And, funders don't want people to fail."

There's a lot of pressure for charities to get everything right all the time. If they're not able to do that, there is a risk that donors might not donate anymore. And people won't show up at their fundraisers. Or they won't get grant funding renewed." I asked, "Isn't that a bit absurd? We know that we need creativity and we need people to do things differently—to come up with new ideas and initiatives. Things don't always work out. Shouldn't we be okay with that?" And she agreed.

So, I shared what the hub has failed at and thought perhaps we should include a failure report in our annual report? We could include all those projects that didn't have good outcomes, all the things we tried that perhaps were risky. She thought that would be an incredible contribution to the city. The Hub should do a failure report. She said, "Trust me, you should do it. You're exactly the type of organization to show people that it's important to be vulnerable. If you're not curious you're not learning and not going to make a major difference."

In 2011, we did our first "failure" report. It rippled through nonprofits across the city, we did radio interviews, and wrote about it. It was an inspirational start to our journey.

Barb thought it was fantastic. She really believed in humility and vulnerability and how important learning is if we really want to see lasting change. We have to be okay with being wrong and being vulnerable and sharing our learning with others.

This experience turned us into a learning organization—one of the core values of the Hub—where you speak and document things that don't work out. It has also influenced the people that use the Hub and helped them to develop their own values.

"Think Big"
Jess Tomlin

LESSON 7
Mission drives success.

MATCH International was founded in 1976 by Norma Walmsley and Suzanne Johnson-Harvor to match Canadian women with resources and resourceful women of ingenuity throughout the world.

The organization sought funding for women to drive change in: health outcomes, reproductive rights, women's political participation, family law, protection from violence, and promoting women's voices at the negotiating table in over 100 countries. It had a beautiful life before it was publicly defunded in 2009, partly as a political decision because of its position on abortion, but also because it wasn't being very well run. Like many Canadian organizations overly dependent on government funding, it had lost its soul and was starting to deliver what the government wanted, instead of what the activists on the ground needed. MATCH was defunded, the organization closed and the staff let go.

In late 2009, a board member, Nancy Gordon, was notified that MATCH had been left an estate gift by a gentleman who had previously gifted MATCH $50 twenty years previously. When I arrived in 2012, it was a bleak landscape for women's rights. What could the next stage of life be for this organization?

It was clear that Canada was not funding human rights work, in particular human rights work being led by women, so we launched the MATCH International Women's Fund, which later became the Equality Fund. At that time the organization was building up from nothing. We had some savings from the estate and thousands of women across the country giving $5 and $10 cheques every month because of the decades of work done by Rosemary Brown, Norma Walmsley and Suzanne Johnson-Harvor.

In that first year we had a $275,000 budget over two fiscal years, and were submitting (perhaps twenty) $5,000 grant applications to activists and human rights movements around the world. It became abundantly clear that our job was to engage Canadians; to get them back to being global citizens who cared about human rights, so that we could move more money.

This is where Barb came in.

I was nervous about meeting Barb when Patricia Harewood introduced us but Barb made time for me. That was her way. Barb was truly "in service" of the work. There was no ego involved. She loved great ideas and an underdog, and was able to envision something before it was fully formed.

I asked if she would join my board when she retired but she said she wasn't joining any board for a year. At her retirement party, I put a reminder in my phone and called her 365 days later. She joined and was really engaged. She was a champion of women, unlocking doors or pre-empting needs with subtle conversations.

Shirley Greenberg was an incredibly generous founding donor. In the early years we had just me and a halftime fundraiser, and we were sending money to Sudan and Afghanistan. Shirley had doubts and called Barb. Barb said, "I trust Jess, and I believe in what they're doing." Shirley gave us a million dollars.

We were working out of a basement in a dingy little office. Barb walked in and said this won't do. You need to be operating on a one-hundred-fold scale to what you're doing in this basement. She introduced me to the President of the Community Foundations of Canada who had space available. Suddenly we had inexpensive but beautiful brand-new offices.

I don't know if Barb actually ever asked for anything. She borrowed on her credibility for MATCH. It was her visibility in front of donors, whether securing a gift, or space, or access. She never did it publicly and never told me she was doing it. I found out after the fact. Even now, I know she helped me more than I'll ever know. She was one of the few people on the board who challenged me

-----

to think as big as possible.

Today, we have 22 employees and $300 million in funding from the Government of Canada, on a path to $1 billion. In 2012, we disbursed $45,000. This year it was $24 million. In seven years, we've come from startup to being one of the largest gender equality funding institutions in the world. On this journey, Barb backed me up, did what she could to open doors and created space and safety. She helped the board see risk in a beautiful way.

She contributed so much to our success. She was completely mission-driven. It was all about the integrity of the work.

You Don't Have to be a Millionaire to Make a Difference
Margaret Torrance

> **LESSON 8**
> Meeting donors where they are, will help to make their philanthropic dreams come true.

My deceased husband Ken was a university professor at Carleton University and we donated to the university before we met Barb in 1999. At that time, we established a donor-advised family foundation. Barb made it very easy for us—even coming to meet us at the National Arts Centre cafe before a performance to sign the papers!

When we began, we would still give to canvassers at the door for heart and cancer month. Barb suggested we direct all donations through our fund at the community foundation. They would send out our donations on our behalf.

We wanted to make an impact with our donations by giving more to fewer charities. To do this, we give all our appreciated shares (outside our registered retirement plan) to our family fund at the community foundation. Charities receive one hundred percent of our donation and government doesn't get 54% off the top in taxes.

Barb enabled the Margaret and Kenneth Torrance Family Foundation to exist. I credit her with making our philanthropic legacy happen. I will continue to manage it until I pass away, and I'm having fun doing it!

We started with five thousand dollars and our fund has grown quite large over the years.

You don't have to be a millionaire to make a difference.

LEADERSHIP

"There are a very small number of people who play influential roles in local corporate, political, community or spiritual endeavours.

The people who cross over these boundaries are even fewer and they are getting older.

Where will we find our next generation of community leaders and how can we nurture them?

In fact, how can we make them even more effective than the generation before?"

Barbara McInnes

Teaching and Leading
Tracy Coates

LESSON 9

You can catalyze change by positively influencing those around you.

I grew up on a farm with few advantages and was by no means wealthy. I left home when I was 16 and lived on the street for a while. At age 22, I left an abusive marriage and started university part-time but joined the student council and became chair of the student charity ball committee.

I worked very closely with Barb McInnes on that student charity ball. She spent a lot of time with me, and I opened up. Barb helped us to see things differently, with a perspective similar to my First Nations culture, which included teachings about relationships and how to mentor—something I'd not experienced in many other places.

She taught us about bias, status and prejudice. She taught about privilege and the importance of having a voice. She did it from a different perspective from our elders. I learned how people articulate ideas in the charity sector. You don't talk about feelings and emotions and relationships the way I was taught. You talk about impacts and capital and economic cases. You conceptualize things in a way that people will understand.

Emotions (that we value from a relational point of view) are not necessarily understood by people who have money and power. So, you must take out the emotion and speak calmly and clearly while still being a woman to be listened to. It was challenging but Barbara taught us through her actions. It was empowering. She took care to analyze how wording in our documents needed to change if we wanted others to hear what we were saying and then invest in it.

Barb went beyond how the gala committee should make donations and what it should do with their funds. She taught how philanthropy works and how society works in philanthropy. Seven of us sat with seven different organizations and were taught how to research, think and to understand change.

We had the emotional energy of youth and we were all women. In the late 1990s there was not a wide range of backgrounds. It was only a few decades into women being able to even go to university. To get OSAP, your parents had to earn less than $40,000. So, you either had to be poor to get OSAP, or you had to have a lot of money and the social support that allowed you to get scholarships. All my courses were homogenized. There was six or seven people in the university who were indigenous. I didn't identify as indigenous then because I had been told that it wasn't a good idea.

Wanting to give to charity was the shared experience that brought us together at the charity ball.

We were interested in human rights and the environment—wanting to make change. Barb explained that you can't give to everybody and idealism wasn't going to get us where we wanted to go. As much enthusiasm as we had, the reality was that how people make decisions is based on bias.

Barb had us study the annual reports and consider administration costs. "This is how much money is going to go directly to animals or single moms." It was brilliant and it was something I didn't learn in my university courses. Three or four of us stayed on the committee the next year…and then the next year, because of Barb. She even acted as my reference to get into law school. Barb made it clear that the charity ball was a special project for her, and that she saw potential in all of us.

Barb provided the foundational tools that I needed to understand and frame things in a different way. She was open to anybody who wanted to be mentored. My relationship with her might seem unique but I suspect that's what she did for everybody. She inspired people to understand and work through differences to create change.

I've had the privilege of teaching social change at university and words like "change-makers" are becoming more common—there are catalysts who create change, (sometimes a lot of change) and others who become the spokesperson for it. Barb catalyzed change through her influence on people like me. In the charity ball committee, she had 5 to 15 young women seeking to create good in the world, who listened to her every year for 20 years. That's possibly 200 young women that she inspired. My generation was the first one to grow up knowing that women are equal and have a voice. In turn, I've learned to teach the lessons that she set the foundation for, to thousands of students.

At the end, we wanted to give her a gift but had no money, so it was a token—costing no more than $40. She replied that *we* were her investment.

I respect all the people who have shared their wisdom with me. I practice Indigenous culture, which has a relational point of view, in my life. Western society has an individualistic point of view so the two may seem incompatible, but they're not. We're supposed to be good people. Barb was a good person and she taught us to be good people. In fact, it was the only thing she asked of us—to be good people. And I've tried my best.

Aligning Values to Action
Zita Cobb

> **LESSON 10**
> *Determination and focus can co-exist with a gentle human touch.*

Barbara and I first met in 2000. I was coming to the end of my career at JDS Uniphase and Barbara was running the Community Foundation of Ottawa. It wasn't until 2014 that she joined the Shorefast Board, the charitable foundation that owns the Fogo Inn and several other businesses on Fogo Island. She was the best board member anybody could ever hope for.

The last time I saw Barbara was in Ottawa, the week before she died. We spent some time together and she was true to form. Barb was one of those people who you could never decide if she was strong and gentle, or gentle but strong. In any event, her strength and the gentleness hadn't changed at all. We had a vibrant conversation about what was happening with Shorefast and on the island and how we were dealing with the pandemic because the Fogo Island Inn had closed. She asked about all the people and how we were going to get back on our feet, so it was quite a "normal" conversation.

I still think of Barbara as I go about our day-to-day work. She was small in stature, but had a steely determination about things she chose to focus on. We just finished our board retreat, an annual event that Barb would have attended, and she was there in spirit.

Returning from being shut down for 15 months has been a tumultuous time. Barb was always the kind of person that you needed to have with you in a tumultuous time, because she had her own North Star, centred deeply at her core. In fact, the more tumultuous things were, the calmer she would get. So, we often invoke her presence.

Barb's love of Canada, and our conversations about our country and our special projects get to the root of my relationship with Barb.

Barb understood that humans are meaning-seeking creatures. We connected on her deep interest and knowledge of art. When I first met her, I talked about this "impossible to believe" island off the coast of Newfoundland and how I thought we could do things that would be good for the island and to create learning opportunities for others. She got behind this idea really, really quickly, and was very supportive of all of the heavy lifting we had to do.

In the last few years, we decided that we wanted to start a community economies pilot project, to try and figure out what Canadians need to do to get the economy working in place-based communities. She instinctively understood our objectives and helped me to convince some of my colleagues that this was important work. The pilot has now launched and we are determined to carry it forward and create a pan-Canadian network for community economies. Without Barb encouragement, I'm not sure I would have taken it the distance that it's come.

A Love for Humanity
Roger Greenberg

LESSON 11
Philanthropy is about providing people with an opportunity to invest in a good cause.

I was born and raised in Ottawa and went to school and practiced law in Toronto.

My dad died suddenly in 1980 and my uncle said "you're leaving your law practice and starting with Minto in Toronto." In 1991, (when I was 35) my uncle Irving passed away and my wife and I moved back to Ottawa, and I became president of Minto. It was a huge responsibility in a difficult economy.

I was very focused on my responsibilities at Minto. My father, mother and uncle were huge believers in the Jewish concept of tikkun olam, which means to give back to the community and participate. My father had been a founder of the Ottawa Jewish Community Foundation before the Community Foundation of Ottawa. After my father passed away, Irving and my Aunt Shirley were very involved in the broader community and the establishment of the Community Foundation of Ottawa Carleton.

Irving had established a scholarship fund for a camp with the Centertown Ottawa Housing at the Ottawa Community Foundation and as I became comfortable with my responsibilities at Minto, I wanted to participate more in the community, so I met with Barb (or more likely, she reached out to me). She convinced me that we should become one of the co-founders of the foundation.

I was familiar with the twin pillars of giving: an endowment where you invest the income, and the flow-through giving in the year it's donated. We had a private family foundation that Irving and my father had set up in the 1970s. When donations couldn't be made for a year or two, many charitable organizations floundered. To borrow from the biblical phrase, you "save up during the seven fat years so that you can continue to survive during the next seven lean years." We've always believed in the duality of both types of giving, current and endowment.

When Barb asked if I would sit on the Investment Committee, I wasn't sure because my experience was in real estate investment. I didn't really have broad experience, but she assured me that it would be a great experience, and they would benefit from having a strong local businessperson. I absolutely loved it. Barb sought input from the committee on foundation policies before they went to the board of directors, and other matters.

I met other volunteers from the community and Gord Thiessen, the former governor of the Bank of Canada, was a terrific chair. After 12 years, I told Barb that I thought we should have someone new. She reluctantly accepted my resignation.

I've had three mentors in philanthropy that helped me tremendously. One was Stephen Victor who asked me to be chair of the new Jewish community campuses in the mid-1990s. The second was Susan Doyle who was president of the Ottawa Hospital Foundation when I joined the first legacy campaign in the early 2000s, and the third was Barbara McInnes. Three completely different people with different leadership styles.

What struck me about Barb was her understated way of conducting herself. It was never about her, and she always maintained that she never "asked people for money"—she provided people with an opportunity to invest in good causes.

Initially, I questioned the sincerity of her statement, but after being around Barb, you couldn't help but realize that she was true to her word. Since then, I've adopted her way as my way—guiding all my activities.

As the chair of the new Ottawa Hospital Civic Campus, we're closing in on $350 million in gifts. Every time I ask to speak with someone about the project, I tell them I'm not asking for money. I ask to talk about an opportunity. Then the decision to give is out of my hands. Barb taught me how to approach people. It was never about her or her ego. Barb was just this pleasant, thoughtful, educated person that had a great way with words, who presented the situation directly.

I'm a competitive person, and Barb wasn't. At her core was a love of humanity and a desire to help those who needed it.

Ask, Don't Tell
Lucy Grossman Hensel

LESSON 12
Engaging donors as "funders" can enrich the philanthropic experience for all.

I grew up in Montreal and then lived in Europe for almost 10 years. My children were born there, and we came back when they were four and six. When I was in Europe, I wasn't giving any money away. It's just so different there. When I came back to Canada, I was giving to my school and to organizations my family knew in Montreal.

I'd been living in Ottawa for about eight years when I realized my charitable donations weren't working for me. I was only giving to organizations in Montreal and didn't know anything about charities in Ottawa. You certainly don't read in the newspaper about such organizations. You read about the National Arts Centre or universities, but not small nonprofits. I wanted to be a part of the Ottawa community. A friend introduced me to Barbara McInnes.

We connected and got along well, resulting in my establishing a donor-advised fund. I realized that the foundation could also help me with my Will, as my children haven't lived in Canada since they left school. When I die, the donor-advised Fund will become an Unrestricted Fund, which is perfect. Flow-through funds also became a good vehicle for me. An invitation from Barb to be a public volunteer on the grants committee was the best thing that ever happened. I learned so much. We reviewed all the proposals and learned about grant making by listening and observing how it all worked and how Barb guided it. It was wonderful.

I don't know which was most important. Letting the grant applicants determine what they needed, or Barb's extensive knowledge of the organizations. The general assumption was that the organizations knew what they needed money for. The foundation did not make top-down decisions. There were no long forms. Applications weren't onerous, especially for small organizations applying for small grants. In the beginning, $400 could change an organization's life. The United Way weren't giving those. I was so amazed to discover a Chinese Canadian organization that required little placards to allow Chinese patients in hospitals to ask for a glass of water, or whatever. It was so basic, and such an eye opener. These were the organizations I wanted to know about. The Community Foundation served many small organizations.

Barb also invited me to sit on a board starting a micro loan fund. She invited me to sit on a panel with two donors at a meeting of Community Foundations of Canada in Kelowna. Our panel was such a success, we did it again in Vancouver. I was amazed that how donor-advised funds were managed in Ottawa was such an eye opener for some foundations. It made me realize how differently Barb ran the Ottawa Foundation. She used donors as funders, getting us more involved and asking what our interests were and what we might like to give to, as opposed to telling us what we should give to. Also, seeing the impact of giving to smaller organizations was both rewarding and inspiring.

Barb was like a fish in water. She was so happy, loving her community and her job. Everyone loved her. Her example was a lesson in leadership and mutual respect. The uniqueness of her approach from other community foundations and her approach to running the grants committee personally helped me a great deal.

She respected the opinions of the people around the table at the Grants Committee. There was no hierarchy. There was no fuss. She listened to everyone and was interested in people's opinions and respected the organizations asking for grants.

She had a huge respect for people who needed money. They came with a need and sometimes a problem, and she would try to think collaboratively about how to best make it work. She made things happen, and she knew the right people. Her agenda was to improve the community, not to make the OCF more powerful, or richer, or bigger. She had an absolute love for the community and the people in the community. She initiated donor site visits and made it all come alive. Under her leadership, giving was more than writing a check.

- - - - -

Illumination as an Approach to Learning
Diane Hodgins

LESSON 13
Collaboration and consensus can be built with positive energy, clear communication and an open heart.

Barb and I worked on several projects together and, on reflection, it was her presence in all these experiences that was truly the gift.

Barb was energy. No matter the situation. No matter the context. Barb brought light, and I don't mean she brought a lightness. She didn't look for a quick fix or put difficult questions aside. Quite the opposite. Barb carried a distinct presence. She knew she was there for a reason, and she took to heart how she could best contribute.

Barb helped everyone in the room see differently by illuminating the space. The positive, the negative and everything in between. She wasn't afraid to tease out what had been left in the dark: the awkward facts, unspoken tensions, poor judgements, missteps, biases or quiet insights waiting to be explored.

She offered visibility and consideration as an approach to learning. She reminded us what was there, what had been built, what we could do, and how we could get there. She was a steady source of energy in the room that allowed things to surface. And her steady energy made every experience better. In a meeting, better questions were surfaced. Better ideas were shared and better opportunities emerged. In a social setting, Barb made everyone feel connected. She found intersections of interest to help shepherd new, and deeper relationships. And, one-to-one, she gave her time and her undivided attention.

She was an exceptional listener and provided an open heart in sharing her wisdom. She cared and you felt it. You did not want to let her down. Barb made things better, and you wanted to be better for it.

You sought Barb out in a crowd. And you always wanted to sit beside her at a meal. She was generous and engaging. Smart and curious. Thoughtful and respectful. Barb could challenge your perspective—but not in a critical or combative way, through illumination. She could show what is rather than what is not and knew how to light up potential.

I became more conscious of Barb's presence while working with a Board subcommittee tasked with reviewing our corporate structure. Committee members had varied depth of related experience, and the content was very technical. It would have been easier, and gone much faster, if Committee members deferred to those with more expertise, leading the others to side with their pre-determined recommendation.

Meeting after meeting, Barb would bring the issue back to centre, putting it among us. No single voice owned the discussion—Barb ensured all were engaged as active participants, even when some were shy speak up. Barb was insistent on an informed, collaborative process; that we left enough space and committed the energy for all to understand the task and bring themselves to it, through whatever contribution they could offer. Barb was a natural developer. She illuminated that the process could not be rushed or directed, and that there was no "right" answer. She was not swayed by tension, egos, or the impatience that arose in the process. Together, we co-created something new, raising our collective knowledge and creating a much simpler, more effective structure than first presented.

Barb was light and when I think of Barb, all I see is yellow—she was an illuminating presence that helped me see differently. Light brings hope and possibility. It brings people together. We all thought differently and behaved better, because Barb was present.

I will forever be grateful for the times I had with Barb, and the masterclass she offered on being an illuminating presence. Barb gave the gift of light, a renewable energy source that is not only transferrable but transformative. In honour of Barb and all she gave to so many, may we all be an illuminating presence for those around us.

Investing in People
Sarah Arden

LESSON 14
Keep an eye on the people and stories behind the numbers. Community service is about connection and relationships.

Barb was the kind of leader who elevated everyone around her, leaving a legacy that transformed both individuals and communities.

I first encountered Barb in 2013 when I joined TELUS as the Community Investment Manager, responsible for overseeing the Ottawa Community Board and its annual allocation of $400,000 in grants. It was an intimidating role, filled with community leaders and seasoned executives, but Barb immediately eased my apprehension with a warm smile, her genuine interest, and a welcoming openness that made me feel like I belonged.

Barb had already been a dedicated member of the board since 2011, and was deeply respected by all who knew her. When she assumed the role of Chair in 2018, her priority was to ensure that the board reflected the diversity of the Ottawa community, and she didn't hesitate to use her expansive network to bring in fresh voices and perspectives. Under her guidance, the board became more representative of a wide array of backgrounds, experiences, and genders, ensuring that the board's support would have the broadest possible impact. This change was a testament to her belief that diversity strengthens communities, and that philanthropy must be inclusive to be effective.

Barb's commitment wasn't just organizational; it was personal.

I remember the times we spent at her home, sitting in her garden with cups of tea or at her dining room table, poring over grant applications and assessing each applicant organization against our funding criteria.

In hindsight they were not just work sessions but life lessons that extended far beyond what we were tasked with. Barb had a knack for inspiring those around her, bringing out the best in others not through authority, but through empathy, insight, and kindness. She cared about the people she worked with—not just as colleagues but as whole individuals. Barb wanted to know who I was beyond my job title: what I valued, what my dreams were, how I balanced life as a wife, mother, and professional. Her empathy and encouragement grounded me, providing a confidence that has carried me through many challenges since.

We worked on numerous community initiatives together, attended countless community events and through our work together on the board, were able to provide support to tens of thousands of underserved young people and families across Ottawa. Yet, no matter how much was achieved, Barb always kept an eye on the people and stories behind the numbers. She believed that community service was about connection and relationships—about investing in people, not just projects.

Beyond her dedication to the community, Barb's love for her family shone brightly. I often looked forward to her stories about time spent with her husband Glenn, their adventures at the cottage, or her pride in her daughters and grandchildren. She was a woman who prioritized family, yet managed to find the time and energy to make a difference in countless other lives. Watching her balance it all made her a role model to me, someone who showed that it was possible to care deeply about community while also making time for people closest to you.

Since Barb's passing, I often think of her in quiet moments—whether I'm swimming in the lake with my own daughters, planning family getaways, or even playing Scrabble, a game she loved. Her memory lingers in these family moments, reminding me of what truly matters. Barb's influence on my life and career is immense, but her true gift was the way she taught me to live more fully, more connectedly, and more joyfully.

Barb facilitated transformation that reached deep into Ottawa's fabric, inspiring others to contribute, to believe in the power of community, and to make a difference. Through her advocacy, Barb fostered a culture of giving where people felt empowered to invest in their own neighborhoods. Her vision brought about programs that continue to benefit the community, from scholarships for local students, to grants for initiatives focused on mental health, social welfare and the arts.

By bringing people together, she left a legacy of change that will inspire generations to come. Her influence is felt in the lives of those who carry on her work, who are inspired by her example, and who remain committed to building a brighter, more inclusive future—one act of kindness, one connection, one shared goal at a time.

A Mentor and a Coach
Manjit Basi

LESSON 15
Find potential in others and then lift it up.

In 1996, Barb called me and said, "I'd like you to join this new initiative to bring a Community Leadership Program to Ottawa." I was 29 and I remember answering, "I don't know how you know me. I don't think I know anything about philanthropy or leadership." Her response—"Manjit, of course you do!" was said in a way that became very familiar over the next 25 years.

Barb was supportive of so many people, but her interest in lifting other women up captures her very, very well. Her ability to see people's potential—especially other women's—was quite incredible.

She believed in people before they believed in themselves and that raises a person's sense of self, and of belonging to their community. Of course, this engages them even deeper in wanting to do more. That's what Barb did for me.

A couple of years later, she asked me to be a member of her board at the Community Foundation, and again I remember saying, "You know I don't fit. I don't even know what philanthropy is. I don't think I'm a philanthropist." I was intimidated so I tried to wear the power suits and carry the briefcase. After the first meeting, Barb said, "Manjit, I didn't ask you to be on the board because I want you to be like everybody else." She truly embraced and affirmed diversity, believing that people's experiences and people's connection to place and community went far beyond the rational thinking that people brought to the table.

One of the legacies that Barb left in this community (and across the country) is that she wanted others to pass on that sense of philanthropy. If you had it, she wanted you to share it with someone else.

I hope I've carried that on in my own way. One of the things I think of in relation to Barb is the Möbius strip, that infinite loop of reciprocity of giving and receiving, because she personified that.

Three Lessons in Leadership
Vinod Rajasekaran

LESSON 16
Lead with curiousity, passion and a bit of mischief.

"A valuable contribution doesn't necessarily need to come in the form of smart answers; it can also be good questions." This was one of the many nuggets of wisdom from Barbara McInnes, a visionary changemaker and one of my most cherished mentors.

People often mention the size of the Ottawa Community Foundation's endowment as one of Barb's big legacies—which was $100 million around the time of her retirement and now stands at $281 million. But in the 12 years that I knew her, Barb rarely mentioned the size of the endowment as a significant accomplishment. She was more interested in finding new, better ways to enhance people's lives.

I met Barb in 2010. I was a young change-maker with a radical idea for the city, trying to feel my way around the craft of social enterprise. I think her first reaction to me was annoyance at my opinions. She had good reason. In those days, I was green and untested. I mindlessly carried around opinions like I carried gum in my backpack. Getting started as a young entrepreneur isn't easy—and getting started as a young social entrepreneur in Ottawa was near impossible in those days. There was no organized community or support. Impact Hub Ottawa—the coworking space and community for change-makers that I co-founded—wasn't just about a bunch of people sharing a printer. I had a vision for it to be a home for people from diverse sectors at a time when change-makers needed connection, knowledge and inspiration. Today, Impact Hub

Ottawa is a flourishing community asset.

Along the way, Barb guided me through some critical choices, and I learned a lot about leadership from her. Here are three of the critical insights I'm reflecting on now.

Lead with curiousity
What she really meant was don't lead with judgement. It's easy to judge people, especially people who have come before you. It's easy to judge people you don't know or don't agree with or might not share the same values as you.

When I was presented with the opportunity to help start up Rideau Hall Foundation as its inaugural managing director, I wasn't sure if I should take it. I had a lot of opinions about the institution. It is, after all, the office and official residence of the Queen's representative in Canada. I had already made up my mind about what Rideau Hall was like, what Governor Generals were and weren't about. Barb encouraged me to *not lead with opinions,* but to be curious about people who might not think or behave like I did. Learn what makes them tick, what gets them excited and what doesn't. She said coming from a place of curiosity rather than judgement means you're carrying an open mind.

Lead with passion
In other words, don't open a conversation with numbers and charts. Graphs and statistics are a newer way of communicating but they don't resonate with everyone. One may think it's a smart way to communicate an idea but graphs can't communicate passion about an idea.

When I presented Barb with the idea for Future of Good, I showed her a bunch of diagrams and numbers, and said this is why it's worthwhile. Barb asked, "Where's the passion?" The irony of course, which Barb pointed out, was that I was sharing an idea for a digital publication without sharing my passion for it through a story.

I was scared of sharing personal stories because I'm an introvert, and an immigrant—English is my second language. I'm also trained as an engineer. None of these things gave me confidence to open up and get personal. Barb pushed me to share my story passionately with everyone: how I was affected, how I was missing out, and how a lack of insightful coverage on social change affected my ability to do really good work.

Lead with a sense of mischief
Have a sense of playfulness in what you're passionate about by taking people out of their routine in a way that helps them do something new or see a new perspective.

When we were developing the inaugural Future of Good summit, we came up with the idea to not share the agenda with participants. We shared general timing for the day but not the panel topics for the keynotes and conversations. I was worried about deviating from the norm so I talked to Barb about it. She thought it was a great idea and encouraged me to think about how to communicate the change as something exciting.

The team ended up talking about the summit like the experience at a concert. You get the ticket and know when it starts and ends, but you don't get a song list. You buy into the experience, fully present, because you don't know what could happen next. It pissed off a bunch of high-profile people who were used to coming and going throughout the day, but when we explained it the morning of, everyone had a good laugh. They got it. The best part was that everyone stayed for the entire summit because they didn't want to miss out on what could be a super interesting talk around the corner.

Barb was an icon of bold humility. She drilled into me that you'll never do anything original and ambitious if you're not willing to be humble. She also taught me that one doesn't need to be loud and boisterous to be seen or heard. She taught me that kindness and compassion matter and that smiles go a long way—because even on a rainy day, everyone in the community can connect to a smile.

COMMUNITY

"The real reason for being, is the impact of the Community Foundation on the life of Ottawa— this city that we love.

Our ability to make timely, thoughtful and much-needed grants is helping to harness and leverage the city's talents, hopes and overall assets."

Barbara McInnes

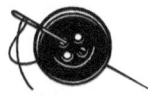

Serenity Renewal for Families
Katherine Godding

LESSON 17
Consider the impact that small charities can have on the community around them.

Ottawa's Serenity Renewal for Families was co-founded in 1983 by a force of nature known as Sister Louise Dunn. After 26 years of helping families struggling with addiction, working out of her south Ottawa convent, Sister Louise was faced with the prospect of seeking outside financial support for the first time. The building was being sold. That was when two kindred spirits finally got to meet, and a whole new vision for the future sustainability of the organization was born.

Sister Louise and Barb were like two long-lost friends. Barb knew all about the mission and enduring impact of Serenity Renewal on thousands of families in the Ottawa area. In 1994, she had funded a program for 26 individuals from aboriginal families in recovery from abuse control and had started paying quiet attention to the work of Sister Louise. As a result, she didn't hesitate in offering her full support to helping it regain its financial footing. She opened doors, helping it to navigate its first foray into the world of community fundraising—leading the way with financial support from the Community Foundation of Ottawa.

My first meeting with Barb took place after Sister Louise's death in 2019, when I was Chair of the Serenity Renewal Board of Governors. We were facing significant struggles restructuring the organization after her passing, including the task of hiring a new Executive Director to guide the organization into the future. Barb offered to speak to the Board, sharing invaluable personal governance and leadership advice that helped set us on a path for success.

At its core, Serenity Renewal has always been a modest organization, never hosting the type of glamourous fundraisers that get written up in the society pages. With an operating budget of less than $500,000 per year, it offers a sliding fee scale to clients, and counts on the generosity of a dedicated volunteer base to run its day-to-day operations. In all her 35 years of leading and providing full-time addiction counselling services with the organization, Sister Louise never once drew a salary.

Barb understood this philosophy, as well as the challenges faced by smaller charities trying to eke out enough funds to carry on with the essential work of caring for the community members in their charge. She recognized the impact made by local organizations like Serenity Renewal for Families, consistently introducing and recommending them to Community Foundation donors and other funders for support. Like Sister Louise, she took a true gardener's approach to community; always nurturing the strengths and virtues of each plant in her care, no matter how modest it might appear. She celebrated and exalted each one for their role in making a contribution to the world around them. She was a gardener of people.

One of the grants Barb supported through the Community Foundation was our B.A.B.E.S. (Beginning Awareness and Basic Education Studies) program that taught 5 to 7 year old children (through puppets and videos) that they are not the cause of problems in a home that is troubled because someone is in recovery from addictions. They learn through storytelling and interactive activities about substance use, addiction, peer pressure, and decision-making, at an age-appropriate level. We try to break the cycle of inter-generational repeat addiction behaviour. The families touched by these types of programs are forever changed.

Most recently Barb was the Chair of the local TELUS Community Board. Although our request was to mainly help adults taking our educational workshops, she understood the ripple effect it had on the families. One person learning new tools effects the whole family. Barb advocated on our behalf and helped us flourish when approximately 80% of people who came to us for support couldn't pay anything for the service they accessed.

People credit Serenity Renewal for Families for, not only saving their lives, but for keeping their families together. Barb helped by encouraging many small agencies not only to survive—but thrive.

Rideau Street Youth
Ken Hoffman

LESSON 18
Respectfully challenging the status quo can lead to innovation and collaboration.

I was a manager in an Ottawa Community Health Centre in the mid-1990s when I met Barb. The focus of my work was community development, and she had started a working group through the Ottawa Community Foundation (OCF) on the topic of "Asset-Based Community Development." This approach supports the sustainable development of communities by focusing on peoples' potential and building on their assets, rather than "fixing" and focusing on their problems and deficits. Barbara wanted to see how we could develop this in Ottawa.

It is, perhaps, hard to appreciate now just how radical this approach was at that time. So many agencies—and especially funders—were fixated on identifying and remedying problems. It was unique to find a funder who was truly interested in working in a different, collaborative way with communities.

This resonated with me and, indeed, served to guide and inform my own approach to community development. It was an approach that inspired me when I worked with others to co-found Rideau Street Youth Enterprises (RSYE), one of Ottawa's first social enterprises. RSYE brought street-involved youth together with local businesses to create opportunities for the youth to re-engage in employment and education, and start to realize their potential. The OCF was an early supporter of RSYE, and Barb provided encouragement and helped make connections to support the work.

Barb used her role at OCF to be more than a funder—she was a catalyst for change. Not only did she challenge the priorities of funders, her work changed the way that funders worked with communities. She had great respect for organizations, like community health centres, who were working on the front lines with the most challenging community issues, and those organizations equally respected her.

Being a change-agent isn't easy. It requires the ability to bring together people (who might view the world very differently) around a common cause. With charm and good humour Barb could help people find common ground. She helped create and nurture relationships and trust, which allowed people to take a chance on doing new and innovative work together.

Although Barb was perhaps best known for her contribution to philanthropy in Ottawa, I would argue this was not Barb's greatest success. There is a quote from Maya Angelou that goes, "I've learned that people will forget what you said, people will forget what you did, but people will never forget how you made them feel." Barb made people feel valued and respected, and with that, it is possible to go far beyond what money can buy.

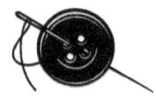

The OCRI School Breakfast Program
Barb McNally and Elaine Garfunkel

LESSON 19
Sometimes having impact comes from connecting others with similar goals and objectives.

We met Barb in the early 1990s when the Ottawa Center for Research and Innovation (OCRI) began thinking about their social responsibility to the community. We wanted our project to be a school breakfast program and had a vision that this was not a school board issue, but a community issue that would require many community partners. We saw OCRI as the lead and other organizations as support partners. Barb agreed and helped initiate outreach to fifteen community organizations.

Barb came to the first meeting with her father Alastair Gamble and Gordon Henderson. We'll never forget it. We explained where we were in the community, what we saw as the growing need, the concept of partnership, and the places at the table. Gordon stood up and said, "I can't believe that there are hungry children in this community. This is Ottawa." After the meeting, I talked to Gordon and Alastair and suggested two or three schools they could visit to see a school breakfast program in action.

At the next meeting we talked about the project again, including potential partners. This time, Gordon stood up and said, "I didn't believe this was a problem at the last meeting. I went to W. E. Gowling Public School and talked to the kids, and we must do this." We were off and running.

Barb would talk to me about her vision for the foundation, and what it could do for the Ottawa community. I wanted to be a part of that vision and became a founding donor. To this day, I still participate and when I pass away, I will leave a substantial legacy to the School Breakfast Program in Ottawa. That's my personal commitment.

Barbara and Gordon Henderson both became big supporters of the School Breakfast Program. Gordon assigned a committed young lawyer, Todd Burke who did fundraisers at the Cercle Universitaire and at Gowling Henderson's offices. Of course, Barb was always behind the scenes making things happen.

I was with the school board for 23 years and the program lasted for 25 years. Later, it became part of "Breakfast for Learning," a provincial initiative. Barb participated in meetings and helped us to build relationships with people who had influence in the community. Today, there are 16,000 kids in the program across the country. When it started, we had 15 to 20 kids per school.

Establishing the breakfast program in schools was a bit delicate. You can't differentiate between "poor" and "not poor" in terms of program participation. Any child was welcome. It was a wonderful opportunity to also ask parents, "would you consider sponsoring another child?" I never had anybody say no.

We eventually got $100,000 in annual gifts from twenty high-tech companies. The Community Foundation was involved throughout. Barb took a real personal interest in our program. She understood it and she supported it, staying involved for many years. If Barb couldn't attend a meeting, she sent somebody in her place. The Ottawa Community Foundation was very hands on. It was an ideal time to connect the business and education communities and other organizations.

Ottawa was the model for breakfast programs across Ontario and Canada. But it wasn't "cookie cutter." Each community had to determine who their partners would be. The Community Foundation put us in touch with people who were interested, and wanted to participate. Barb called it convening; bringing people together.

The Founding of PAL Ottawa
Jim Bradford, Jim McNabb and Victoria Steele

LESSON 20
When possible, adopt a whole community approach.

In 2012, a group of artists and friends of artists in Ottawa, assembled to investigate a plan to establish a live/work residence for aging members of the local arts community. Barbara McInnes was the first community leader to step forward to offer help and advice.

We, as a society, reward artists with applause and appreciation, and we often assume that success in the arts brings financial security. However, very few members of the arts community arrive at the end of their career with either an adequate pension or financial resources to meet basic needs. Patterned after PAL (Performing Artist Lodges) in Toronto, Vancouver and Stratford the vision was: "Seniors residing in the National Capital Region who work(ed) in the arts sector to be assured access to affordable housing and personal support in a creative, caring communit—so they can continue to live, create and inspire."

Ottawa joined the PAL family in the Fall of 2012 with a launch at the Ottawa Art Gallery. Barbara took out a membership and enthusiastically told her friends. The Community Foundation also engaged by investing in a pivotal feasibility study.

Barbara, and her husband Glenn, continued their incredible support for PAL Ottawa by opening their home for PAL's first Garden Party fundraiser in September of 2013. The McInnes' art collection made this a very attractive venue for the event which had a large attendance and included many community leaders. Their kitchen was the centre of preparation of many treats for the guests and the backyard the focus for a dance performance by members of the Ottawa Dance Directive. Inclement weather kept the guests out of the garden, but they watched in awe through the windows as the performers donned rain gear and filled the space with movement. A sizable amount of money was raised that day and we knew that our plan was possible. In 2023, shovels broke ground and the plan became a reality.

Barb was steadfast in her support, serving on PAL's Advisory Committee for many years giving advice on strategies for business models, potential partners, political support, and fundraising. A longstanding arts supporter, she was well aware of the needs of the artistic community and its important role in the wellbeing of the Ottawa community as a whole. Her concern for the entire community was founded on the firm belief that a strong and dynamic community comes from cooperation and integration of its many parts.

A Vision of Community
Alex Munter

LESSON 21
Ideas, fueled by passion and accountability becomes a sustained vision for change.

In the early 1990s, I was in city government. I had heard of Barbara and clearly recall the first time I met her in person. She was a small person physically, but came into the room like a whirlwind—with ideas of what needed to be done and how I could help.

This would have been in the early years of the Community Foundation of Ottawa. When, in many ways, it was still just an idea. Barb turned this idea into a remarkable force for good in our community. It reflected her personality and energy, her passion to make a difference and her ability to connect people and ideas with programs and organizations.

After I left city government, I sat on the grants committee of the Community Foundation and Board of Directors for a few years. Most funders have narrow criteria; organizations compete for funds and must meet funders' requirements.

Barbara was a fierce protector of the Community Foundation's resources. She set very high standards for what she would fund, yet at the same time she did not impose a lot of rules and restrictions. She was all about results—

- *How can we make things better?*
- *How can we use community foundation dollars to create change and attract other funding?*

She loved this community. She wanted to make things better for people and was always trying to figure out ways to do that. She was a remarkable person and I learned so much from her.

Barb had a vision of a community that is just and fair—where there's opportunity, where there's joy, where art flourishes, and where children can play and thrive. She devoted her life to making those things happen and it was never about her. With humility and determination, it was all about making our community stronger and better. Not in some theoretical or rhetorical way but in looking for practical, realistic ways to help organizations succeed. The goal was to expand the number of people the Foundation could serve and to make every dollar reach its maximum impact.

Barb was always direct. She loved to travel and a few years ago I shared my itinerary with her for a trip to Burma. She said, "No, don't go to those places—they're boring. You must go to Inle Lake." I'd never heard of this community built entirely on stilts in a lake and it's hard to get to. Nevertheless, we went there and it was one of the most meaningful travel experiences of my life.

When I think of Barb, I think of Ottawa. I think of the countless people who never knew her name but whose lives were improved by her work. I think of Inle Lake. I think of her laugh. I think of that larger-than-life spirit that still brings a smile to my face and always will.

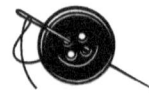

A How-To in Community Building—Kindness as a Constant
Yasir Naqvi

LESSON 22
Philanthropy intersects with community through the work of community foundations.

I met Barbara McInnes after I was elected as a member of Provincial Parliament when I was still in my early 30s. My constituents were mostly in Ottawa's Centertown area, not the entire community, as is the case now.

It was in the beginning, getting to know and meet people, that I was introduced to Barb. I was immediately struck by her kindness. She didn't judge. She also didn't overly praise. Her kind approach was consistent—the same every time we met. That kindness meant a lot. It gave me confidence. It made me feel like I belonged.

I was new to Ottawa when I first ran for public office, but Ottawa was my home and I had something to contribute to the community. Wanting to build a better community was one of the reasons people elected me, but having a sense of belonging is intangible and comes from acceptance.

Now, I've become part of this community, and nobody doubts my affection or connection to it. Barb was one of the people who made that possible.

Community building through community foundations, where philanthropy intersects with community, was something that I learned from Barb. I didn't know the ways community foundations used money (without judgment) to help shape a community. Now, I am exposed to community foundations from all over the world, but it was Barb who first introduced me to the concept.

OTTAWA COMMUNITY FOUNDATION

*"In building this organization,
we are leaving a legacy
that will serve the community in more
important ways every year.*

*Long after we are gone,
our work will make a difference in the lives
of those we will never meet."*

Barbara McInnes

A Primer on Community Funding
Catherine Dubois

LESSON 23
The grants program at the Ottawa Community Foundation led with trust and a transparent process of decision-making.

I first met Barbara at a conference offered to Ottawa agencies working in the not-for-profit sector. Like me, many of the participants looked forward to this annual conference as one of the few professional development opportunities open to us at the time. Funds were rarely available for front-line workers in grass roots organizations to learn or share best practices away from the job. Sitting in a crowded classroom, I was struck by Barbara's key messages, delivered in a kind and thoughtful tone.

Barbara spoke about the value of staying true to our mission and to never succumb to pressure to shift from our mission to accommodate funders. She congratulated our organizational efforts to reflect the diversity of the communities that we served, but made it clear that we were barely beginning as a sector to take the necessary steps in hiring, mentoring, acknowledging and embracing leadership within the black, Indigenous and multicultural communities. To that point, she ensured that a sister panelist, a black woman with extensive research on Ottawa's BIPOC community, was invited to present her findings in an atmosphere of welcome and warmth.

Please note that this dialogue took place years before diversity, inclusion and representation became a priority topic in any meaningful public forum in Ottawa.

Several years later, I was able to join Barb's team managing the Grants Program at the Ottawa Community Foundation. The best way to sum up this experience would be to call it a primer on community funding. Her bar for excellence was set on fairness, rigorous research on funding applications, complete alignment with a transparent process of decision-making, and a shared aim for excellence. She invited staff in all positions to attend Board meetings and Board Committees. It was not unusual to witness meetings when administrative assistants would sit at committee tables with the CEOs of national and international financial institutions. She wanted her colleagues to have every advantage to learn, to observe, and to be part of a wonderful team.

She started every single day with a walk-around, (it was like a light being turned on) but some of my favourite moments were spent driving to visit community organizations with Barbara. She used those moments to teach me, to provide context, to fill in lines with a lifetime of experience in building a better community.

Without exception, Barbara would be welcomed on these visits with genuine pleasure. She was a diminutive woman, but was lifted up by the respect and love people had for her. She trusted community organizations. It was a mark of this trust and esteem that she would caution against reducing grant amounts from the amounts entered on funding request budgets. She believed that if an organization asked for a certain amount, then they needed exactly that… and probably more.

To contribute to Ottawa's efforts to tackle longstanding gaps in services, Barbara launched Ottawa's Vital Signs, an annual report card of key indicators on how Ottawa was thriving or lagging behind in critical areas; such as the gap between the rich and poor, the wellbeing of residents pertaining to health or their sense of belonging, safety concerns and the importance of arts and culture on city-building. This accessible resource became an invaluable asset as organizations and funders worked together in new and innovative ways to focus their efforts on tackling the problems identified in Vital Signs. This, in turn, provided much-needed momentum for evidence-based positive change.

Later in my career I worked as an executive director in a community resource centre. My days were long, and my job duties ranged from strategic planning to resolving plumbing disasters. There was rarely a time when I did not reach for the tools that were so gently placed in my toolbox by Barbara, to:

- *be fair*
- *bring people in from the margins*
- *show up every day with heartfelt intentions and energy*
- *trust in the power of community development*
- *listen carefully to many diverse voices*
- *shine the light on all the good work of others happening every day*
- *be pragmatic about all the vagaries that so challenged me*
- *to take care of myself, to the same extent that I tried to care for others*

I mourn Barbara. But it is impossible to dwell in loss when I have such gratitude for her presence in my life. She sought the good in every person she met, and in every organization she supported through the Community Foundation. She found the good, and for me and countless others, *she* was "the good." The very best.

In Support of Visual Arts Organizations
Julie Hodgson

LESSON 24
Lead by example.

In 2010, after a career at the National Gallery of Canada, I retired and joined Guy Bérubé at Ottawa's La Petite Mort Gallery (LPM) where I launched the LPM Collectors' Group, I organized events once a month, with tours of public and private art collections and talks by guests who spoke about art and collecting, conservation, lighting, design, framing, installation, art appraisals, and the media among other topics.

When the LPM Gallery closed in 2015, I wondered how to continue supporting visual arts organizations in Ottawa and met Barbara McInnes, the CEO of the Ottawa Community Foundation.

The Ottawa Community Foundation answered all my questions.

Barbara certainly led by example. She told me to:

> *Talk to people about your fund and the work you are doing, and don't be afraid to ask if they'd like to donate and/or if they would like to be involved.*

> *Offer options for involvement and suggest a donation level. E.g. the average donation is $250. Involvement might be simply signing up for the series, or it could be contacting someone they know who might offer to invite the group to see their art collection.*

> *Ask people who are already donating and/or participating if they know of anyone else who might like to donate and/or be involved. Many of the people who signed up for the Ottawa Talks Series were friends of people who had signed up for the series. Word of mouth certainly helps.*

I set up the Ottawa Art Society through the Ottawa Community Foundation as a nonprofit, charitable organization. To promote the Ottawa Art Society, build our endowment fund, finance our annual grants, and provide an educational program from our Members, I also started the Art & Architecture Series in 2017, featuring tours of public and private art collections and architectural spaces.

Barbara led me through the process. It was incredibly easy to get started and was very much in line with my desires to support the visual arts community in Ottawa, and to leave a legacy. I was deeply touched that the first donation in the amount of $1000 came from the Barbara McInnes Community Fund. I felt incredibly supported and on my way!

Also, following Barbara's example, I became involved with two mentoring programs, including the Carleton University Practicum Program and the Ottawa Community Foundation to learn about their work and organize fundraisers in support of the Ottawa Art Society.

To date, we have provided grants of $2500, with our first grant in 2016 going to the Ottawa Art Gallery Expansion Fund.

City of Ottawa Poverty Reduction Committee
Michael Maidment

LESSON 25
Hard work today can have lasting impact into the future.

My story started at the Salvation Army. I was responsible for Community Family Services programs which focused on homelessness, housing, addiction, rehabilitation and poverty relief, and was also the volunteer chair of a City of Ottawa advisory committee on poverty. While I didn't have a lot of interaction with Barbara at the Community Foundation, she asked me to join the committee she and Colleen Hendrick, who was head of city social services, were co-chairing. We worked over two years on one of the first poverty reduction strategies in Canada.

Barb put together a comprehensive group. The business sector was represented by Jeff Dale, the head of OCRI. She felt strongly that school boards be represented, because we needed to think about kids. She formed a cross-sectoral group to develop a strategy for council to endorse with a budget. We made 16 recommendations which were practical and would benefit the city. Then, it went to council, was endorsed in the Spring and then there was an election in the Fall. Jim Watson was elected mayor and unfortunately set the Poverty Reduction Strategy aside. Jim's focus was more on rent supplements.

Our debate had been about who was responsible for reducing poverty. Is it organizations like the Community Foundation, or the Salvation Army or homeless shelters, or others working in that space? Or is it the provincial government? In the end, the municipal government always points to provincial government, and the federal government says we can't really do anything. Our report recommended several practical initiatives, that could be done. It wasn't an aspirational document. It set out concrete actions we could take as a community, without asking for more from the provincial or federal government.

Fifteen years later another poverty reduction strategy meeting was cohosted by the city with the community. Again, there is a conversation about the need for a coordinated approach and strategy for poverty reduction. I suggested we should look at the good work done in 2009. This may result in resurrecting initiatives that were never acted upon and could still make a big impact.

In 2013, the Ottawa Food Bank was seeking a new CEO. I had been in the nonprofit sector for seven years and wanted to lead an organization, but I wasn't sure I was ready. I called Barb for an opinion. She was encouraging, giving me guidance and the confidence that I was ready to apply. And she acted as a reference. I feel I got that job because Barb was standing behind me. I held that position for seven years. My vision at the Food Bank grew out of my work with the poverty reduction committee and the belief that we could do better for people facing poverty.

Now I am leading the Ottawa Community Foundation. It has been a full circle for me. I witnessed Barb's leadership that impacted so many organizations and people and was excited to follow the person who was responsible for me becoming a CEO and who successfully led the organization for so many years. She still lives in this place. Her name is brought up often. My approach to the work is very much aligned with how she did this job. She remains a mentor for this organization.

If Barb hadn't chaired the poverty reduction committee, I don't know that there would've been a committee. The city needed somebody to lead the committee who the sector respected and knew could get something done. It was Barb and her relationships in the community that gave it momentum and produced a strategy. It was an impressive work effort that still stands today.

It Began with The Nominating Committee
Gordon Thiessen

LESSON 26
Excellent board members will lead to strong and effective board governance.

I met Barb McInnes for the first time when I found myself having to chair the Nominating Committee of the Community Foundation of Ottawa. In conjunction with the founders of the Community Foundation, one of my predecessors, Gerald Bouey, had committed Bank of Canada governors to carry out this role in perpetuity. I knew little about the Community Foundation and wondered how I could possibly ensure that the Nominating Committee would make good choices of board members. Barb McInnes, in her wonderful way, quickly put me at ease. She described the contribution of the Foundation to the Ottawa community and the role of the Board so clearly and passionately that I became an immediate convert. The candidates that Barb recruited and brought to the committee for consideration were so impressive that choices were not difficult.

Barb kept in touch with me after I retired from the Bank. At that point Gerry Bouey was the chair of the Foundation Investment Committee. As my longtime mentor, Gerry would often tell me about the Foundation and that I should consider it as an interesting and rewarding activity for my retirement but it was not until 2008 that I agreed to join the Investment Committee and eventually become the chair.

I quickly realized how important the Investment Committee was to the success of the Foundation. As Barb and other board members and supporters attracted new donors, the resulting larger investment portfolio allowed the committee to include a wider range and more complex types of financial assets and become a stronger and more reliable generator of income to fund the Foundation's many grants to the Ottawa community.

I also learned just how important the Foundation was and how successful it had been. It was clear that the nomination process and Barb's recruitment of excellent board members had led to strong and effective board governance at the Foundation.

I was interested in becoming a donor but was hesitant because I thought that the Foundation might have been designed mainly for large donors. Barb and I had a quiet conversation where she rather gently persuaded me that my wife and I could begin as small donors and add to our fund over the years just as she and many others had done.

The Growth of the Ottawa Community Foundation
Peter Doherty

LESSON 27
It's not difficult to manage money when everything's going well. A community foundation has a fiduciary responsibility to serve the community in good and bad times.

I was involved with the Community Foundation from its inception until I retired.

The Community Foundation of Ottawa-Carleton began with a half-million dollar bequest and endowment fund from the United Way in 1987. An Investment Policy was developed from the beginning. It was accelerated when interest rates were high to keep income flow high to optimize what we could give. The investment portfolio was focused on fixed income and we considered whether more equities would be appropriate. We grew slowly from the first million. It took several years, and we maintained a fixed income until the portfolio reached $5M. Once it hit the next threshold, we knew we could pay a permanent staff person. Alastair Gamble and Barb didn't get paid for years.

Our goal was to grow our assets, so we had enough to give to the community and pay our staff. This led to conversations about the role of the Community Foundation as a philanthropic service for the Ottawa community. Our growth had to be managed with some delicacy, particularly with the United Way.

Barb was fabulous because she was never a threat in the community. She was diplomatic with everybody and was able to articulate how the organizations could collaborate with each other to serve the community without giving up their independence.

The principles of governance were developed early and were progressively well-articulated as time went on. Good governance put the Community Foundation of Ottawa on the right road from the beginning.

We were sensitive that the Foundation could appear to threaten organizations soliciting donations to do good in the community. We were careful that our governance model recognized the role of other philanthropic organizations in the community and not something that would divert funds from them.

Barbara and I talked about the role of equity in our investment portfolio, and the proportion of equity gradually rose with diversification. The balance of reward and risk was prudently considered in recognition of how the community needs money the most when the world is in upheaval. It's not difficult to manage money when everything's going well. Our attitude was that a community foundation had a fiduciary responsibility to serve the community in good and bad times.

Just after the high-tech meltdown in 2000, Barb and I were at a Community Foundation of Canada meeting in Vancouver with many Community Foundations from across North America. American foundations, in particular, had experienced a huge drop in value. We expected to talk to people whose portfolios had dropped by 10-15%, but there were 50% drops and, in some cases, higher.

Our investment and governance policies meant our loss was significantly lower and we were able to continue to give grants to the community from our assets until our earnings bounced back.

P. J. Doherty managed the fund for several years free of charge. Eventually we charged a fee 25% lower than our standard. This continued to my retirement and—to the best of my knowledge—continues to this day.

I was also involved in the creation of a Financial Advisory Committee which produced a financial advisors guide. This committee was formed so that financial advisors could advise people how to do philanthropic giving. Barb became the first person who was not an estate planning lawyer or accountant to become president of the Estate Planning Council.

It was apparent early on that Barb was very talented and a force to be reckoned with. Barbara was extraordinarily good with donors. She cared more about people than their money. A Community Foundation is a giving committee to a geographic area where there are needs, and people trying to service the needs. It was an easy board to be on because there was a shared understanding of what we were doing.

Ottawa needed somebody capable like Barb, because we'd see organizations asking for money that were delivering the same service. They may have been in different neighborhoods, but they were doing basically the same thing. They viewed each other as competitors. The Community Foundation got them to recognize that they were all trying to achieve a common goal and that they were better off using synergies rather than operating independently. They let Barb paint that picture.

As the Foundation grew so did its visibility and influence in the city. There were never any fights over who should get credit. The whole organization always got the credit. The Ottawa Community Foundation also led the national growth of Community Foundations. They were instrumental in creating a national organization; creating and defining its raison d'etre. Then, they allowed it to evolve as things became more complicated.

The other beautiful thing that occurred is the increase in the amount of capital. It's now an engine; a huge influence in Ottawa for grants for charitable organizations. It's developed an excellent method of attracting new donors because of the skillful way they've funded the community and the way grant giving is perceived by both the recipients, as well as the donors. Their investment policy and grant giving program has been managed well over the years. It's got all the things that make it a well-run organization, without bias or privilege.

Thirteen Years of Service on the OCF Board
Maureen Appel Molot

LESSON 28
The rules of governance are critical to any well-functioning organization.

I still remember the call in 1992 I received from John Crow (Governor of the Bank of Canada) asking if I would accept a seat on the Ottawa Community Foundation. I knew a fair bit about the OCF and its contributions to the wellbeing of many in the City of Ottawa because Barbara McInnes had been a friend for many years. Her enthusiasm for what the foundation was accomplishing knew no bounds.

I came to the OCF after many years as an active volunteer in the Ottawa Jewish Community. In my 13 years on the foundation board, I was privileged to: Chair the Grants Committee, to serve as OCF Vice-Chair and then Board Chair, and finally Past Chair.

The Grants Committee
The Grants Committee, comprised of a few board members and a number of knowledgeable Ottawa citizens met twice yearly to assess applications for funding and to make decisions on which organizations would receive support. Barbara participated in meetings of the Grants Committee. Her wide knowledge of the voluntary sector in Ottawa made her presence in the group invaluable. As the Committee debated the merits of an application Barbara would often provide relevant background information on the agency behind the application

or insightful comments about what the innovative approach the head of the agency was taking in serving those it supported.

As foundation assets increased so did the amount of money we could allocate. Some of the funds under the foundation's stewardship were dedicated, e.g., the income marked for an Ottawa hospital or the Boys and Girls Club. But most funds were not restricted, which meant the Grants Committee had considerable discretion in making its granting decisions.

There was no end to compelling applications for support from a huge range of community organizations in the city. What struck me each time the committee met was the breadth of applications that came from agencies in social services, the arts and culture, education, the environment, and health. Barbara often met with organizations which the foundation had not yet funded to encourage them to seek support. It was her community activism that generated applications from Indigenous groups, and from some of the social service agencies serving newcomers to Ottawa.

Governance
Not long after I'd joined the board, Barbara raised the issue of "governance" at one of the regular Board meetings, suggesting it was time for the CFO to review whatever rules of procedure were then in place, make any changes deemed necessary, and consider areas that thus far had not been addressed. While perhaps not as interesting or inspiring as grantmaking, rules of governance are critical to any well-functioning organization.

Among the topics that fall under the rubric of governance are the terms and selection process for board members, the size of the board, procedures for the selection of the President and CEO, potential conflicts of interest, procedures for CEO succession—whether the need to replace the CEO was sudden or planned. Of the wide variety of things that I did while on the CFO Board, learning about governance was one of the experiences that had the greatest impact on me.

Community Foundations of Canada
Barbara's commitment to the community foundation movement extended far beyond the borders of Ottawa. She was an early advocate for the (then) relatively new Community Foundations of Canada (CFC). For many years the CFC had an office at the CFO. When I joined the CFC Board, I spoke with many

community foundations professionals from across Canada, who raved about Barbara McInnes' immense contribution to the national association. In fact, Barbara's reputation within the expanding world of community foundations led to the CFO being one of only three Canadian community foundations invited to participate in the first Symposium on a Global Movement held in Berlin, Germany in December 2004.

Participants from every continent discussed the challenges of philanthropy from their specific country perspectives and how to increase it. Barbara was an articulate advocate for the Canadian community foundation movement and for the lessons learned around growing philanthropy in a city based on the CFO model.

Over many decades I've learned a huge amount about philanthropy—how to make a difference in a community's well-being, how to encourage philanthropy and to create foundations which generate resources for charitable giving into perpetuity, and a bit about philanthropy outside Canada. I owe most of what I know to my time at the CFO and most definitely to my long and close relationship with Barbara McInnes. She left us far too soon.

From Intern to Staff at OCF
Gillian Whyte

LESSON 29
Working directly with donors allowed the Ottawa Community Foundation to quickly respond to urgent grantee requests and community emergencies.

While working as an administrator at Carleton University in 1998, I applied, and was selected for, a mid-career internship in philanthropy at the Community Foundation of Ottawa. I was excited at the prospect of working in the field, because at that time there were no formal education options for learning in that area.

I worked directly with the President, Barbara McInnes, whose passion for community was evident from the beginning. As I followed her from meeting to meeting—with donors, grantee organizations and community leaders—I was in awe of her compassion, community knowledge and boundless energy. When it came to addressing specific issues within the community, Barb was always willing to take the lead, and was brilliant at bringing all the right people and expertise to the table. I learned so much during this time just by listening and observing Barb in action.

After completing my internship, I was hired by the foundation into the role of donor services and continued to benefit from Barb's mentoring for 13 years. During this time, Barb continually challenged me by expanding my role and responsibilities, which included asset development and managing a large portfolio of donors, memorial funds, scholarships and educational award programs. There were also a number of special projects assigned to me, including organizing the Transatlantic Community Foundations Network visit to Ottawa and conducting research into best practices and innovations in asset development and donor engagement.

Barb was an excellent mentor and role model who was generous and giving of her time. She ensured that the Foundation was always ready to respond to urgent grantee requests and community emergencies by working directly with donors to secure the necessary funding, thus allowing everyone to work together to address the city's most pressing needs. I believe this was one of her greatest gifts and it left a lasting impression on me, as well as a legacy that the entire city continues to benefit from.

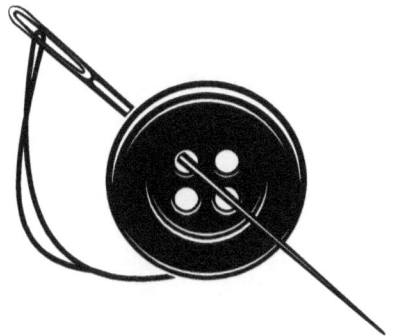

BEVOND BORDERS

"Reaching out into the community, creating and maintaining connections, especially at the neighbourhood level, is what we do best.

Yet, we draw strength for this grassroots work from our national and international connections.
We continue to learn from best practices elsewhere.

A great strength of the community foundation model is that it's not a stagnant institution, but is constantly reinventing itself to address new opportunities and challenges."

Barbara McInnes

Building Community in Eastern Europe
Ian Bird

LESSON 30
Doing the right thing in the moment, with a focus on relationships, has an enduring effect.

While recently attending a conference in Bucharest, I couldn't help but reflect on the impact that Barb's mentoring has had on Eastern European countries.

Two hundred people with a shared sense of common agency were attending the conference. Much of the Ukrainian leadership found their way to Romania, despite their current wartime experience. There was enough maturity in the room to not demonize Russia, and not paint everyone in the context of Russia with one brush because we all understood that there's a lot of work going on below the radar. Conflicts always have layers.

An ecosystem of community philanthropy leaders attended the conference to work on "what's required right now, within my sphere of influence" alongside the notion that "we're going to shape a generation."

As I met people for the first time, they asked, "Oh, Ian, where are you from? Wow, you're not far from Ottawa. Did you know Barb McInnes?" "Of course, I knew Barb," I'd say. "In fact, I coach her grandson."

Tipping the Dominoes
Barb's efforts in Eastern Europe were at one end of a chain of dominoes, similar to her work in Ottawa. It's was *her* first set of relationships that tipped the dominoes that allowed me to show up years later, and have a conversation with

someone whose geopolitical situation is very different than ours.

I try to imagine a community in Hungary with 15,000 people, and 7,000 refugees arrive in a matter of months. Fortunately, there's a core civic infrastructure to respond to that situation and it stems from those early conversations initiated by Barb and others. If Barbara was here today, I imagine she would say, "Oh, but we just did this thing. We can't lay claim to those future achievements." But the reality is, that's what's played out. If Barb hadn't been in Eastern Europe 25 years ago what I experienced at the conference wouldn't have existed.

It should encourage today's leaders to pause and think—to what extent are we successful in spending time in deeper relationships? We can have some confidence that such achievements can be transformative. It's made *me* think very differently about what a community foundation is. Most people focus on a community foundation as a mechanism for philanthropy, or the means for donors or grant making to flow resources to important work. But it's more important to see it as a critical *infrastructure* that has a long, enduring effect.

Consider a community foundation like other infrastructure we may take for granted—such as systems to bring water into our homes. Our water systems are not just so we can have a glass of water; they are for overall health. That's what was going on when Barb first went to Latvia. It's not the water going in and coming out the tap, it's a way of looking at that infrastructure.

Barb was always working towards the broader health of society. Why is that important? Physical health comes from access to drinking clean water. In the same way, community health comes from having access to abundant relationships and all the resources which promote a healthy society.

There I sat in Eastern Europe, on the border of conflict, and there's a community foundation infrastructure with its leaders reflecting on what, why, and how they're doing it. It's an echo from conversations that started with a handful of people around a table in Latvia, with a mission-critical agenda of the wellbeing of Eastern Europe a generation later.

Enduring Unforeseen Outcomes
Barb would be embarrassed to be represented as a solitary agent in this achievement. It didn't happen that way. It wasn't just her in a relationship. She

was linking up and creating a multilateral world, creating a multiplicity of contributors that resulted in the outcome I saw in Bucharest.

But many similar efforts have failed in the past because the people that did the initial work felt they needed to hold it, or own it or be it. They didn't make space for others to come in and bring their gifts.

So, that's another one of Barb's achievements. Her way of going about it—making connections and crowding people in around things in a way that became the ethos of the Community Foundation. It dismantled the sense that people needed to distinguish themselves by doing their own thing. They were distinguished because they joined in the cause. The great community foundation leaders—Barb's peers, didn't focus on money. It was the human component. The ideas. The sense of collective agency. The working across differences.

There was no Canadian "plan" to expand community philanthropy into Eastern Europe but it wouldn't have grown without those initial meetings. Barb's approach created what we now have—where I can walk into a conference room in Romania as a part of ongoing international work. There's now an expansive network of community foundations in Eastern Europe that were nascent when Barb was first there.

I want to say she planted seeds, but that's not the right word. "Planting seeds" might be interpreted as knowing or anticipating that the plant would grow in a certain way and become a certain thing. That wasn't what Barb's achievements were predicated on. Rather, it was the result of Barb having her hands in the dirt with others, and working through what was important at that moment.

Barb's work led to sustained relationships. People exchanged experiences, and came and visited one another, and participated in each other's activities.

Now—in this moment—in the Ukraine and Russia and bordering countries, we have a network of community foundation leaders who are intimately involved in peace movements in Russia, in community redevelopment and emergency response in Ukraine, in refugee support and in community philanthropy.

I must emphasize how present Barb is *today* in Bucharest—a place most of her community of friends, colleagues and collaborators would probably know nothing about. There I was attending a gathering of folks with genealogy back to those initial conversations and relationships started by Barb in Latvia. Within a span of just a few decades they're doing aligned work with a passionate commitment to community and mission. That's what endures. Me, showing up as a Canadian, brought Barb into the room. Her connection tied me in.

West-Vlaanderen Community Foundation
Jan Despiegelaere

> **LESSON 31**
> Community foundations are about human capital; working with people—donors and grantees—to find the best possible way to invest in potential.

I came from the private sector and found working in philanthropy to be strange. It's a magnificent field, but we also tell each other how good we are and how wonderful we're doing, and how smartly we see our community's needs and the impact our changes make. I'm a pragmatic, critical thinker, and sometimes people are not critical about what we do because "it's a good cause for the community."

Barb could be both inspirational and pragmatic and she was not a missionary for community foundations. Based on her example, I try not to put myself or the community foundation first. Instead, I like to see how others can have their own role and place. An important thing I learned from Barb is that modesty is key to how our foundation operates and how we work with others.

The Game-Changer
Barb and I had a meeting with Luke, my chairman who was CEO of a big bank. He was absolutely engaged and motivated, but quite focused on the numbers. He had a hard time getting a clear picture of how to run our foundation. Being president of a charity was more abstract than he was used to. We had no unique selling proposition or market. Luke asked Barb, in very bad English, why should donors and partners work with our community foundation? Barb said, "you're a banker so you understand capital and assets but it's not about numbers. When

you are the president of a community foundation, it's about human capital."

She went on to explain that community foundations work with people—donors and grantees—to find the best possible way to invest in potential. It can be financial, ideas, expertise, or it can be issues close to their hearts. You can build with this kind of human capital. This is how we differ from a charity or service club, or from other foundations.

I saw in Luke's eyes that he got it and it completely changed how he perceived our organization. In that moment I thought, "this is very important, this has even more potential on a national and European level. This is really what it's all about."

I still use "human capital" as my baseline. As a phrase, it has convinced other entrepreneurs, major donors, and philanthropists to start their own community foundations in Belgium and other regions of Europe. This was the language; this was the picture and it was so easy. It took no longer than five minutes to explain that a community foundation involved long-term investment, not quick play or transactional management. Some community foundations are transactional and some manage funds from multiple donors in different areas. There are also community foundations trying to evolve and manage and operate as human capital investment funds.

Barb's contribution that day made a huge impact. She made it clear that we're pioneering a new field where you must adapt to your own community. She created confidence in me (and a whole new generation) in community foundations as a concept.

The template was context-based, *not* what works in Canada. It was informal teaching. (In fact, this also taught me that informality was more powerful and impactful than other things I had learned from other community foundations.

Barb pointed to the horizon and gave me the confidence and opportunity to try things that didn't fit a formal template. There is a quote by Proust, "The voyage of discovery lies not in seeking new landscapes, but in having new eyes."

Community Foundations of Canada
Richard Mulcaster

LESSON 32
Act locally, think globally.

The Council on Foundations in the United States has held annual conferences in various cities where—over three days—we could interact with other community foundations of comparable size dealing with the similar issues.

The Canadian community foundations attendees would find themselves at these events with 800 or 1000 attendees, where we would meet and have a glass of wine on one of the evenings and talk about things that were happening in Canada. Many of our challenges were different than in the U.S., and it was great to speak with others about the Canadian experience. At that time, The Community Foundation movement in Canada was not connected in any way, and at first, we were all just conference friends. Then, in Seattle in the late 1980's, Barbara and the rest of us began to think about the idea of creating a network of Community Foundations in Canada.

At the Seattle conference, we got together in somebody's hotel room, to discuss how we could help emerging community foundations, and create new ones in Canada. Certainly, Barbara and Alastair Gamble believed that a Canadian organization was required. I remember Barb saying, "as Community Foundations we need to act locally, but we should think nationally and internationally." This idea took hold. We organized a planning committee for a constitution and a corporate structure for a national membership organization.

Then Barbara said to the group, "I think Richard should be the chair of the planning committee because he is the CEO of the largest foundation." I was honoured to take that role and over the next year Barbara and Alastair and I did a lot of work. Alastair travelled across the country, meeting mayors and developing an interest in community foundations in both small and large towns. The commitment from Barbara and Alastair in Ottawa inspired the rest of us. The McConnell Foundation provided startup funding and people like Jamie Laidlaw from the Laidlaw Foundation and Michel Lamontagne from Montreal, and others in philanthropy, became connectors across the country. People could see the vision, support it and be enthusiastic about it—and so it grew.

We launched Community Foundations of Canada (CFC) in Ottawa on April 5-7, 1990, at our first national conference. A foundation volunteer, Anne Bouey, chaired the conference's organizing committee. It was an outstanding success bringing together approximately 100 representatives from 32 established foundations and 13 interested in exploring the concept. The conference eventually culminated in the formal founding of Community Foundations of Canada in Winnipeg in 1992. Barbara joined me on the founding Board at the first meeting in Winnipeg, along with Dan Kyayfeld from Winnipeg, Marjorie Sharp from Toronto, Wayne Stewart from Calgary, Bob Siskind from London and Kent Newcombe from Hamilton.

The Vancouver Foundation board believed it was an interesting idea but thought the focus of community foundations should be on "community," and this was a national idea. I was very enthusiastic about it and convinced my board to become a part of the national organization and financially support it. Our chair, Tom Rust became inspired by Barbara's and others energy when he attended the initial meetings. Barbara had a spark for inspiring people.

I remember sharing a taxi to the airport with a group (including Barbara) after one of our CFC meetings. Someone said, "I've never been a part of setting up a national organization, it's very complex and it takes a lot of work." Barbara said "Yes, but everybody grows into these things and someday we'll look back and say this was a piece of cake." We hoped Barbara was right, but all saw it as a very large multi-layered and multi-flavoured cake. But Barbra was right, we all did grow into it and her logic stuck with me.

The Community Foundation of Canada has had an interesting evolution. We envisioned a purpose, and did what we thought we could do at that time, and it has evolved to where it is today.

It went further with the advent of the Transatlantic Community Foundation Network. We had conversations about why we should focus our energy internationally. We believed it was our turn to lead, and that we had something to lead with. We discussed how community foundations in Canada had grown with the support and assistance of foundations in Canada and the U.S. and it was our turn to step up and participate in an international forum.

The Bertelsmann Foundation in Germany believed that the creation of community foundations could make a significant contribution to philanthropy in Europe and particularly in Eastern Europe where it could help post-communist countries create a civil society. Bertelsmann formed the Trans-Atlantic Community Foundation Network and asked Community Foundations of Canada to contribute to the creation of an international model. The American model is great, but Canadians have a different style of leadership, and CFC could present a different, and in some cases better, model for other places in the world. So, Community Foundations of Canada helped bring a new concept of philanthropy, through the Transatlantic Community Foundation Network to Europe and also Mexico.

There are many European and quite a few Mexican foundations now that resulted from the Transatlantic Community Foundation Network. The decisions of the board, that Barb and I were so much a part of, gave the community foundation concept a local, national and international perspective.

Those experiences gave us energy, increased vision and a broader scope. Our international connections helped us with our work locally. We were mentoring and learning at the same time. We shared our experience, and learned what philanthropy and volunteerism meant in post-communist countries in Eastern Europe.

We laid the foundation for what exists today.

Massawippi Foundation— No Giving Up
Margot Graham Heyerhoff

LESSON 33
Modest beginnings can lead to great things.

I'm a founding member of the Massawippi Foundation and a trustee of the Massawippi Conservation Trust. We set out to be a Conservation Trust but decided we didn't want the trustees to be worrying about fundraising—we wanted them to concentrate on acquiring land, either by donation, servitude, or purchase, and to concentrate on maintaining that land once it was protected.

The idea of linking up with a community foundation came from another founding member, Thomas Wilcox, who was the President and CEO of the Baltimore Community Foundation. Tom knew the foundation world and suggested that we have a community foundation manage our money and grant funds to the trust, (which was its own registered charity) and other charitable entities around Lake Massawippi. With this purpose, member David Rittenhouse began a search.

The Sherbrooke Foundation, though local, was just getting established. The Montreal Community Foundation required everything to be endowed with no flow-through capabilities and they couldn't help our American donors get a U.S. tax receipt. The answer was the Ottawa Community Foundation. They could work bilingually and had 25 years' experience and a reciprocal agreement with the New Hampshire Community Foundation so Americans could receive a tax receipt. It was a great fit. In September of 2010, Patterson Webster and David Rittenhouse drove to Ottawa to meet Janet Adams, and established the fund.

We met Barb later. She and her husband Glenn had been on a trip to Thailand (coincidentally, with my brother Ron Graham and sister-in-law). The day after Barb discovered the connection, she came for tea with some of our board.

At that meeting, Barb shared about the early days of the Ottawa Community Foundation (OCF). Her inspiring words that day really made a difference. She encouraged us—telling us stories about how the OCF had started with no money, holding lunches to meet people in the community and tell their story. It was exactly where we were. We had very little money. We had very few people interested in knowing about us. Barb's story inspired us. I said, "There is hope that we will grow, that we will survive, that we will protect land, and that we will be able to give grants. We just have to give it some time and keep working and not give up."

And here we are. We set up a big tent in a field with a farm-to-table lunch to celebrate our 10th anniversary in 2020 and to launch a capital campaign. Now, we have $6.5 of our $7 million capital campaign goal. The trust has protected over 1,400 acres of pristine, ecologically important land; some of that purchased by our fund at the Ottawa Community Foundation and we have more land coming. We're going to double our acreage by the end of 2025. The trust has built 18 kilometers of natural trails within the conserved land we funded—trails that were so important for people's well-being during COVID. And, we have a talented board of directors.

University students use the land for research projects. For example, there's one going on about the Northern Dusky Salamander. The Foundation also funds an education program with hundreds of young students in grade four to six who visit our conserved lands. We have a professional outdoor educator, who the foundation pays for, as well as buses, snacks, and porta potties. Our fund has helped to protect the land and provide research, education and recreation—the four tenants of conservation.

We've surprised ourselves by our success, and the fact that we're widely known and respected. This started with a link to the Ottawa Community Foundation with Barb's inspiring words guiding us to where we are today.

The Community Foundation of Hanover
Dorothea Jäger

LESSON 34
Connect donors to projects.

In English we are the Community Foundation of Hanover, but in German there is no word for community, so we used "burgers" which means citizens. We're the foundation of several citizens.

The Bertelsmann Foundation, with support from the Charles Stewart Mott Foundation, created the Transatlantic Community Foundation Network (TCFN) in 2000 to serve as a platform for the exchange of knowledge between North American and European community foundations.

I attended the first Transatlantic Community Foundation Network plenary meeting in 2000 in Dresden (in the Museum of Hygiene). Barbara and I were in the same working group, where we studied endowments, fundraising and donor services. Our group met several times over three years in Dublin, Milan, Florence and Vancouver, learning how community foundations functioned and about each other. We were just starting out and related to the Canadian model. It was not easy in the beginning, and Barbara's encouragement helped change my perspective.

We were one of two community foundations in Germany. Hanover and Gütersloh. We were invited along with Nikolaus Turner, the Managing Director of the Foundation Lindau Nobel Laureate meetings.

I had the pleasure to again be in the same working group with Barbara for a second three-year term with gatherings in Mexico City, Newcastle, Baltimore, Dublin, Ottawa and Brussels. Learning from the experience and know-how of more established community foundations was very important, and the relatively young Community Foundation of Ottawa offered a good model to me and our Community Foundation of Hanover. Barbara helped us find the right bearing.

TCFN held a conference in Ottawa in 2001 that included site visits showing the impact of her foundation's grant-making in Ottawa. We met with dedicated, caring and enthusiastic board members doing very meaningful work. These learnings were a very convincing influence.

Barbara coached me when we weren't reaching our goals and had people on the boards that were not so helpful. She helped me design a vision that clarified the kind of people we should take on. With that vision, we achieved great success. We started with 50,000 euros in 1997 and in 2024 we have an endowment of 36 million euros.

The advice from Barb was to find the "right people" for the board; to have paid staff; to fundraise for operational costs; to build "donor service" by offering donor-advised funds and to involve donors in the grant-making process. Oh yes, and to take donors on site visits. I strove to follow her good example and have fun doing it!

At the annual conference of the German Council on Foundations in Freiburg in 2004, Barbara presented a paper on the growth cycles of community foundations that included the opportunities and dangers and problems of each growth phase. This presentation was widely regarded as the tool for thinking about and acting on, the "growth cycles of a community foundation." I'm still learning from it, and we will reach the prime life cycle!

Donor-advised funds were recommended by Barbara based on how she, herself worked. It turned out to be very impactful advice. In Canada, her donors were well-connected to the projects with site visits. Similarly, we invited our donors to see schools or special new clubs or creative arts organizations or music schools for unprivileged people to show donors how much joy their donation was bringing to the organizations. Donors increased their funds because they were thrilled by what they saw. The first donor-advised fund we set up was our own family and company donor-advised fund. Today we have almost thirty donor-advised funds and more than 50% of our endowment is donor-advised funds.

Building Communities Nationally and Internationally
Monica Patten

LESSON 35
Building authentic relationships will result in trust.

Barb deeply understood the concept of community. She knew the neighborhoods in the City of Ottawa and the surrounding region. She knew that community was about people and relationships with people. And, she understood that within those relationships, there were different communities of particular interest groups: for example, the arts community or the LGBTQ community or even neighborhood associations. Her understanding of community was put into practice every day. She knew the way to engage with any community was through the relationships that she developed. She put time, energy and skill into relationship-building and the result was trust.

Barb had the trust and respect of everyone she worked with. She worked to solve troubling aspects of a relationship until she determined how to make it stronger. Barb was deeply, deeply connected to the community. It was who she was—her personality, her style. She also valued learning. She brought John McKnight to Ottawa to talk about his book "Building Communities from the Inside Out" and his understanding of the usefulness of neighborhoods' local resources, capacities, and relationships. Barb learned from him and with him. She read his writings and invited others to learn from him.

This work and understanding of community guided her work nationally with the chief executives of community foundations throughout Canada.

She knew that leadership, in the form of Community Foundation of Canada learning sessions, was a shared responsibility. But she also offered constant leadership to the network of 10 or 12 foundations. Barb was always present, never missing a gathering and was generous in her time and what she shared, and in listening to others, even when there wasn't always agreement. Barb never insisted on "her way" and she was equally generous with smaller community foundations in Ontario, and beyond.

Barbara built a model for community foundations that the broader community appreciated. A community learns and is inspired in many ways. Barb's honesty and straightforward approach garnered respect. She didn't pussyfoot around and was thoughtful in how she gave feedback and comments. And, she was inspiring. That is what made it work. Community is never built by one person but building trust and developing enduring relationships contributed to her accomplishments and the development of community and the community foundation in Ottawa and across the entire country.

This was her great commitment to Canada and to the community foundation movement. She was a builder.

Barbara made time to attend the Transatlantic Community Foundation Network meetings and was in constant communication between meetings. She'd get an email from a friend in Poland, or from Germany, where they were beginning a community foundation in their own vision. It didn't look like the Community Foundation of Ottawa, yet they'd want to test an idea or ask a question. Her international work was very important to her in her own modest way. She would say, "Yes, I'm helping Dorothea in Germany, but I'm learning from her too." Then, she'd pass on the wisdom she gained with her home community.

Initially, Barb worked with colleagues in the United States to bring the community foundation movement to Canada. Over the years, Canada chose its own path, putting an emphasis on building community and on granting. We became more comfortable with relationships in Canada. The differences with our neighbour to the south astonished Barb, who represented us often in the United States. She'd come back and say, "I just don't get it. All they think about is …." She always had a loving, but slightly critical relationship with her American colleagues who valued what she had to say, because Canadian foundations were similar to the U.S. but with core differences.

Barb was beloved by many. She was kind. She was thoughtful and she was supportive. She was all the things we think of as being a "nice" person: well-informed, a good listener, generous, gentle. But along with that niceness, she was also intelligent. She knew what she wanted to accomplish and never lost sight of her work. She wanted a community where people shared a generosity of spirit in the community and her vision enabled her to stimulate action and activity, e.g. inner-city health in the early days. Her route may have changed along the way as she met people and formed partnerships because she knew when to say to recipients and donors, "Come with me," or "Can I come with you?"

Barb believed that a community foundation Executive Director's role should be on the street, not in the office. She would say, "I've just had a meeting and was so moved by that person's story." She was respectful and in awe—not of money—but of the thoughtfulness and generosity of those she met and was committed to bringing their intentions to life. It's never easy to be an organization asking for money. We all know that. I've been a grant maker and a grant seeker and there is a power imbalance.

Barb made it easy for grant seeking organizations to ask for money while never compromising on the principles and the rules and the community foundation guidelines. She would never act unilaterally, only with the support of others. She understood the dynamic but cared more about the people than their money.

Community Foundation for Ireland
Tina Roche

LESSON 36
Start by listening.

I founded the first Community Foundation for Ireland as the CEO in 2000.

Ray Murphy, who worked for The Atlantic Philanthropies, rang me to say that an organization called the Transatlantic Community Foundation Network (TCFN) was coming to Ireland, with CEOs of community foundations from America, Canada and from Europe. Was I interested in meeting them? I said I would absolutely love to meet with them, but more than that, I would love to sit in on their discussions, because we had never seen a community foundation in action. I'd only read about them.

The first day I met Barbara and said I didn't know anything—literally, I just knew the name "community foundation." She insisted I stay, and I did—for four days, sitting in the back taking notes while they discussed what a community foundation was. Barb was brilliant, because she'd stop, look at me and ask if I understood what she meant. She was helpful from the word go, and we just clicked. On the third night, I organized a drink at a pub and there was dancing. It was just a magic night; we had such fun.

Barb insisted that Bertelsmann include me in the Transatlantic Community Foundation Network. We were just starting, with only our name and an endowment of 400,000 Euros. We'd given out only 80,000 Euros a year. I said, "Barbara, we haven't done anything yet, we're literally starting off." Her reply was that we could learn from everybody else's mistakes.

The next year TCFN invited me to visit the New York and Baltimore Foundations in America. Every time I ran up against a problem, I would ask Barb what she would do in this situation? Bertelsmann generosity brought experienced people like Barbara and other CEOs of foundations in the States and Canada to people in Ireland, UK and Europe and Asia who were just starting. It put an engine behind the work that we were doing. And through TCFN I met everyone in the UK.

Our board was considering what to do about our investments. Do we put our investments into social impact, or do we put them into equities? Barbara said she would have a discussion with the board, but Barbara ended up doing one better. The chair of her board had a long discussion with our chair, who made the decision to put 10% of our endowment immediately into social impact. It took quite a while to determine where to invest. Canada was way ahead, with organizations that told you how to invest, and did due diligence. In Ireland, we didn't have that infrastructure.

It took a while for the seeds Barbara planted to flourish in our foundation. Our grant making is now between 20-25 million euros every year, with an annual endowment of about 60 million. We have a lot of flow through. Our donors give about three million euros a year. It's doing extremely well.

Barbara didn't just work with us, she worked with many community foundations in Eastern Europe, and even Russia. Barbara offered transformational leadership in the transatlantic community foundation network. She gave her knowledge freely and would listen to what anybody's issues were. She would say, "I can see your problem and we don't have that in Canada. What if we looked at it this way?" When I joined in 2000 there were 800 or 900 foundations and now there are 2,100 in Europe. This is her legacy.

- - - - -

CONTRIBUTOR BIOS

Medin Admasu
Youth in Philanthropy (Lesson #4)

Medin believes strongly in the Boys and Girls Club (BGC), especially for young people and their families living in low-income housing and its' impact on the lives of children and youth across Ottawa. He has worked in the not-for-profit sector for 25 years starting as a locker room attendant at the BGC, then as Program Coordinator, Youth of the Community Foundation of Ottawa for two years, then Tenant Community Worker for Ottawa Community Housing Corporation for five years, then as a Program Manager with the Ontario Trillium Foundation and now as the Chief Programs Officer with the BGC.

Maureen Appel Molot
Thirteen Years of Service on the CFO Board (Lesson #28)

Maureen served as Chair of the Community Foundation of Ottawa from 2003 – 2005, as a member from 1993 – 2006, and then served on the board of Community Foundations of Canada. She retired after 33 years from Carleton University in 2006 as the former director and Professor Emeritus of The Norman Paterson School of International Affairs. Maureen received the Gilbert Greenberg Distinguished Service Award in 2013 from the Ottawa Jewish Community. She was the first woman president of the Jewish Community Council of Ottawa.

Sarah Arden
Investing in People (Lesson #14)

Sarah has spent over two decades fostering community impact through philanthropy and partnerships. In her first six years at TELUS, she managed the Ottawa Community Board, working with senior community leaders to distribute grants to local charities. She now works on the TELUS Corporate Events team, often planning events with a charitable focus, including TELUS Community Board launches and the TELUS Friendly Future Foundation Gala. Previously, she held roles at The Conference Board of Canada and CHEO. Sarah has volunteered with local charities, including The Ottawa Mission, Ottawa Children's Treatment Centre, and other youth-serving organizations.

Manjit Basi
A Mentor and a Coach (Lesson #15)

Manjit weaves people, ideas, and perspectives to build more connected, compassionate communities. For 21 years, her four Body Shop franchises served as hubs for ethical business, learning, and belonging. She's chaired Immigrant Women Services Ottawa and served on boards including the Community Foundation of Ottawa, Elmwood School, and Rideau-Rockcliffe CHRC. A founding member of Leadership Ottawa, she also hosted a Rogers TV series spotlighting changemakers. As Synapcity's founding director, she sparked cross-sector dialogue to bridge divides. Today, she coaches teams to unlock their collective potential and deepen their impact. She also chairs the Telus Ottawa Community Board and HP Ward Foundation and sits on the board of the Centre for Social Enterprise Development.

Ian Bird
Building Community in Eastern Europe (Lesson #30)

Ian competed in field hockey in the Summer Olympics in 1988 in Seoul and 2000 in Sydney. After reaching his personal athletic goals as a two-time Olympian, Bird used his love of sport and sense of public responsibility to support a larger vision of building resilient and inclusive communities as President and Chief Executive Officer of Community Foundations of Canada from 2011 to 2020, the first Executive Director of the Rideau Hall Foundation, and Founder and Coach of the Phoenix Field Hockey Club in Chelsea, Quebec. In 2024, he became CEO of Community Foundations Australia.

Jim Bradford, Jim McNabb and Victoria Steele
The Founding of PAL Ottawa (Lesson #20)

Performing Arts Lodge (PAL) Ottawa's mission is to connect members of the professional performing and allied arts community, mainly seniors and disabled members, with essentials such as affordable housing, personal care services, and links to the local arts community, so they can live, not in fear and hunger, but in dignity within a caring community. It was founded 12 years ago by Jim Bradford (Chair), Victoria Steele (Treasurer) and board member Jim McNabb, among others. The Ottawa PAL with 86 affordable apartments for older artists will open in 2026.

Tracy Coates
Teaching and Leading (Lesson #9)

Tracy is a part-time Professor in the Institute of Canadian and Aboriginal Studies at the University of Ottawa specializing in law, indigenous knowledge, and community mobilization. Tracy is of mixed Mohawk and European ancestry from an Urban Aboriginal Community and holds a Juris Doctor from Osgoode Hall and a Masters in Environmental Studies from York University. She has been a Program Advisor in cultural competency and Aboriginal program development with the School of Social Work at Ryerson University and the School of Public Policy and Administration at Carleton University, and served on the legal teams of the Assembly of First Nations and Amnesty International Canada.

Zita Cobb
Aligning Values to Action (Lesson #10)

Zita is an eighth-generation Fogo Islander. After the collapse of the inshore cod fishery, she attended Carleton University, then worked at Ottawa-based JDS Fitel for ten years becoming CFO of JDS Uniphase until 2001, when she exercised her stock options, and sailed around the world for four years. Zita established the Shorefast Foundation on Fogo Island in 2004 with her brothers Alan and Anthony Cobb. Shorefast opened the Fogo Island Inn in 2013, a 100% social enterprise, with all surpluses reinvested in Fogo Island through Shorefast. She is also the Fogo Island Inn Innkeeper. Shorefast has created The Shorefast Network for Place-Based Economies, "to figure out how other communities across the country can build up local economies rooted in the particulars of a place."

Jan Despiegelaere
West-Vlaanderen Community Foundation (Lesson #31)

Jan has a Masters in Political Sciences and has been the general coordinator of the Regional Fund West Flanders, managed by the King Baudouin Foundation, since 2004. He is also working on the Foundation's "Local Strategy" and has always been an active participant in several international groups and networks, such as the late Transatlantic Community Foundation Network (TCFN). Jan is co-founder of MyMachine, an internationally acclaimed initiative dedicated to promoting creativity in education in 12 countries.

Peter Doherty
The Growth of the Community Foundation of Ottawa (Lesson #27)

Peter founded the investment counsel firm Doherty & Associates Ltd. in 1979. With over $2 billion in assets under management, the firm manages foundation, trust and investor portfolios. He was a founding member of the board of Community Foundations of Ottawa-Carleton, Ottawa Financial Analysts and governor of the Camelot Golf Club. In addition, Peter was a Director of the Estate Planning Council, the Rotary Club, the Victorian Order of Nurses and Ottawa Executive Association. Peter sat on the Board of Morison Lamothe Inc. and the family Service Centre of Ottawa, Carleton University and was Co-Chair of Royal Ottawa Hospital building Committee.

Catherine Dubois
A Primer on Community Funding (Lesson #23)

For over thirty years Catherine has helped people overcome the barriers of the social determinants of health: meaningful employment, affordable housing, education, economic stability, healthcare and a sense of belonging in community. She worked for the Eastern Ottawa Community Resource Centre, South East Ottawa Community Health Centre, and as Executive Director of the Rideau-Rockcliffe Community Resource Centre. She has been a Board Member of the Ottawa-Carleton Independent Living Centre, Maison d'Amitié, Operation Come Home and volunteered at Bruyère Health, Emergency Food Cupboard, Lowertown Community House and Blair Court Community House. Catherine is a Recipient of the Joan Gullen Annual Award for Advocacy.

Katherine Godding
Serenity Renewal for Families (Lesson #17)

Katherine Godding, a lifelong resident of Ottawa, has dedicated over 25 years to health and fitness, with a deep passion for the connection between physical and mental well-being. She has volunteered with Serenity Renewal for Families for over a decade, serving as Chair of the Board for two years, and has supported the Taggart Family Y for more than 20 years. Through her work and volunteerism, Katherine strives to give back to the organizations that have given so much to the community, helping individuals and families find strength, resilience, and well-being in their daily lives.

Margot Graham Heyerhoff
Massawippi Foundation—No Giving Up (Lesson #33)

Margot was a Founding Trustee and Chair of the Massawippi Foundation in 2011 and is currently President and a Trustee of the Massawippi Conservation Trust. Margot served on the Bishop's College School Association Board of Directors from 2003 to 2009. In 2004 she became President of the North Hatley Library Association, a position she still holds. She is a Founding Director of the N'Oubliez Charitable Foundation and in 2023 was honoured with a Doctor of Civil Law (Honorary) from Bishop's University and awarded a King Charles Coronation Medal in 2025. She is a supporter of Bishop's University's Sustainable Agriculture and Food Systems and its Educational Farm.

Roger Greenberg
A Love for Humanity (Lesson #11)

Roger has been with the Minto Group for 40 years and is currently the Executive Chairman of the Board and has been the Executive Chairman and Managing Partner Ottawa Sports and Entertainment Group for 11 years. He was Invested into the Order of Canada in 2013 and was awarded the Ottawa Chamber of Commerce Lifetime Achievement Award in 2014, the Outstanding Volunteer Fundraiser by the Association of Fundraising Professionals in Ottawa in 2010, Volunteer of the Year by The Ottawa Hospital in 2008, the Ottawa Jewish Community Gilbert Greenberg Distinguished Service Award in 2007, Ottawa Business Journal CEO of the Year in 2004 and Community Builder by United Way in 2001.

Lucy Grossmann-Hensel
Ask, Don't Tell (Lesson #12)

Thinking outside of the box. Innovation. Empowerment. Adaptation to rapid change and an interest in bringing about sustainable, transformative change to our communities, guides donor Lucy. She has helped fund over 50 local initiatives and groups such as iSisters Technology Mentoring, Pathways to Education, Centretown Laundry Co-op, Eco-Equitable, the Wabano Aboriginal Health Centre, OCISO and the City for all Women Initiative. She served on the Ottawa Community Foundation Grants Committee from 1998 to 2002. Lucy participated in the planning of the Ottawa Community Loan Fund which was established in 2000 and continues to assist those who are not eligible for traditional financing.

Diane Hodgins
In Support of Visual Arts Organizations (Lesson #24)

Diane is Executive Vice President of Shorefast, an innovative social enterprise based on Fogo Island, NL building models to catalyze place-based economic development across Canada. She was appointed Chief Financial Officer of Shorefast and the Fogo Island Inn in 2015 and Director, Investment Partnerships of Shorefast in 2012. Diane was with Ginsberg Gluzman Fage & Levitz, LLP from 2000 to 2012 and JetForm from 1997.

Julie Hodgson
Illumination as an Approach to Learning (Lesson #13)

Julie has been an Exhibition Project Manager for the National Gallery of Canada, Portrait Gallery of Canada, Canadian Museum of History and Canadian Centre for Architecture. She's volunteered with Festival X: Ottawa's Photography Festival, Ottawa Blues Festival and the AIDS Committee of Ottawa, among others. She's the past Chair of the Advisory Board of the Carleton University Art Gallery and was on the Boards of the Ottawa Arts Council, Ottawa Community Immigrant Services, and the Coalition of New Canadians for Arts and Culture. She retired from the National Gallery of Canada in 2010 and began a Collectors' Group and set up an Ottawa Art Society Fund at the Ottawa Community Foundation.

Ken Hoffman
Rideau Street Youth (Lesson #18)

Ken has worked and written about community development in Ottawa for over 35 years, including as the Director, Community Health Promotion, Sandy Hill Community Health Centre (1992-2002) and co-founding Rideau Street Youth Enterprises (1995-2010), a social enterprise to provide employment and education opportunities for street-involved youth. He is currently a partner with One World Inc., a consulting firm that supports engagement between governments and the not-for-profit sector. One of his current passions is using photography to tell the story of community development initiatives in Canada and abroad.

Jackie Holzman
Plant an Acorn (Lesson #1)

Since the 1950's Jackie has made a difference. Whether it's Ottawa Para Transpo, the Jewish Family Services, Causeway Work Center, Salus, Tamir and Rehab Institute housing, Royal Ottawa Hospital, Ottawa Health Sciences Centre, Ottawa Hospital Breast Health Centre, Rehab Centre, planning for Unitarian House, Temple Israel and many more, all before she was elected to City Council in 1982 and in 1991 through 1997 as Mayor. In 1997, her volunteer activities continued at the Community Foundation of Ottawa, Ottawa Congress Centre, National Capital Commission, Canadian Cancer Action Network, Ottawa Hospital Research Institute, Ottawa Kiwanis Club, Honorary Lieutenant Colonel of the Cameron Highlanders of Ottawa and co-founder of Compassionate Ottawa. Jackie's volunteer work was recognized by Algonquin College, the University of Ottawa, Volunteer Ottawa, and the Sovereign's Medal for Volunteers.

Dorothea Jäger
The Community Foundation of Hannover (Lesson #34)

Dorothea has a business degree from the European Business School, Oestrich-Winkel. As one of 31 citizens in 1997 (during her maternity leave) the Jaeger Group GmbH family business donated capital to start the Community Foundation of Hannover (Bürgerstiftung Hannover), a citizen-driven organization focused on fostering civic engagement. Dorothea served on the board for 10 years, then as chairwoman from 2007-2023. She applied what she learned in both stages of TCFN to help the Community Foundation of Hannover grow to what it is today. Dorothea is a fan of contemporary art and the Sprengel Museum Hannover, which ranks among Germany's most important museums.

Michael Maidment
City of Ottawa Poverty Reduction Committee (Lesson #25)

Michael was appointed President and CEO of the Ottawa Community Foundation in 2023. Previously, Michael led the Ottawa Cancer Foundation as President and CEO and the Ottawa Food Bank as CEO. He was a member of the roundtable that helped develop Canada's first legislation on Human Trafficking, the former chair of the City of Ottawa Poverty Issues Advisory Committee and helped develop Ottawa's Poverty Reduction Strategy in 2010. Michael was the chair of Feed Ontario, a board member of Orkidstra and the Crossroads Children's Mental Health Centre, and currently serves on the board of the Mississippi River Health Alliance.

Elspeth McKay

Operation Come Home (Lesson #2)
Elspeth was the Executive Director of Operation Come Home from 2007 to 2022 and is now an Executive Advisor. Elspeth has worked tirelessly to advocate for homeless youth and those that are vulnerable in our community. She is highly regarded for her community economic development activities and the development of social enterprises. Elspeth recently won the King Charles III Coronation Medal for her community work.

Barb McNally & Elaine Garfinkel
The OCRI School Breakfast Program (Lesson #19)
Barb retired as Vice-President of the Ottawa Centre for Research and Innovation Ottawa in 2003. For 20 years previously she taught secondary school and was then seconded to Bell-Northern to promote activities linking business and education. Barb has volunteered with the Elizabeth Fry Society.

Elaine launched the school breakfast program in 1990 in one school, which expanded to 91 schools, with over $2.5 million raised to feed almost 6,000 children. She is a founding member of the Teddy Bears' Picnic Committee of the Children's Hospital of Eastern Ontario and has helped raise money for the Queensway Carleton Hospital Foundation through the Kanata Kountry music festival.

Russ Mills
Leveraging and Multiplying Good (Lesson #3)
Russ joined the Ottawa Citizen in 1971 where he became Editor and Publisher of the newspaper. He also served as President of the Southam Newspaper Group. In 2002 he received an Honorary Doctor of Laws degree from Carleton University. He was a Nieman Fellow at Harvard University in 2002-2003. He joined Algonquin College as Dean of the Faculty of Arts, Media and Design in 2003 and became Chair of the National Capital Commission in 2007. He also served as Chair of the Community Foundation of Ottawa, Chair of The School of Dance and President of Michener Foundation for public-service journalism.

Wendy Muckle
Turning Good Ideas into Reality (Lesson #5)
Wendy started in nursing 1981, then in 1990 worked with the homeless with the City of Ottawa and the Sandy Hill Community Health Centre. She co-founded Ottawa Inner City Health in 2001 and retired in 2022. She hopes her appointment to the Order of Canada in 2024 is for being a "good citizen of Canada and of the world." Since retirement, she has volunteered with Block Leaders, engaging homeless people from the drug using community. For the past 20 years, Wendy has worked in Kenya helping transform the lives of widows and orphans through education and community economic development.

Richard Mulcaster
Community Foundations of Canada (Lesson #32)

Richard Mulcaster spent 25 years with the Vancouver Foundation, serving as Program Director for a decade and as President & CEO for 14 years. After retiring, he held leadership roles with the Justice Institute of British Columbia, the University of British Columbia, and The Arthritis Society, BC & Yukon Division. He has also contributed to organizations such as the TELUS Community Board, Arts Club Theatre Foundation, Canada World Youth, and the InnerChange Foundation. Now fully retired, Richard spends much of his time cruising the West Coast of British Columbia aboard his 32-foot Tollycraft, enjoying life on the water.

Alex Munter
A Vision of Community (Lesson #21)

Alex has decades of experience in the health and social sector. He became CEO of the Canadian Medical Association in 2024, from 2011 to 2024, he served as president and CEO of the Children's Hospital of Eastern Ontario. Prior to CHEO, Alex served CEO of the Champlain Local Health Integration Network and as Executive Director of the Youth Services Bureau. He was an Ottawa City Councillor from 1991 to 2003. Alex has been a member of the boards of the Ontario Hospital Association, Children's Mental Health Ontario, Kids Health Alliance, the Children's Aid Society of Ottawa, the Community Foundation of Ottawa and the Ottawa-Carleton District Health Council.

Yasir Naqvi
A How-To in Community Building—Kindness as a Constant (Lesson #22)

Yasir was elected the Member of Parliament for Ottawa Centre in 2021. He was Attorney General of Ontario while a Member of Provincial Parliament in Ontario for 11 years. Yasir was the CEO of the Institute for Canadian Citizenship from 2019 to 2021. He's a strong believer in community and the importance of giving back, and has sat on the boards of OrKidstra, United Way East Ontario, and the Ottawa Local Immigration Partnership. He was called to the Ontario Bar in 2001 and immigrated to Canada from Pakistan with his family in 1988.

Monica Patten
Building Communities Nationally and Internationally (Lesson #35)

Monica Patten was President and CEO of Community Foundations of Canada from 1993 to 2011. During that time, she was active in the development of global community philanthropy, serving as Chair of WINGS (Worldwide Initiatives for Grantmaker support), a board member of the Global Fund for Community Foundations, an advisor to the Transatlantic Community Foundation Network and a Synergos Fellow. Monica, a Trudeau Foundation Mentor, was appointed to the Order of Canada in 2013. Now retired, she is an active volunteer in Ottawa, including as Chair of Compassionate Ottawa.

Vinod Rajasekaran
Becoming a Learning Organization (Lesson #6)
Three Lessons in Leadership (Lesson #16)

Vinod is Publisher and CEO of Future of Good, a digital publication covering the social-impact world. Previously, Vinod was the founding Managing Director of Rideau Hall Foundation, chaired by former Governor General David Johnston. Vinod was also the Co-founder and Executive Director of Impact Hub Ottawa. He launched Canada's social R&D network as a Fellow with SiG and the McConnell Foundation. Vinod was designated a Global Shaper by the World Economic Forum, a winner of the Lewis Perinbam Award for social innovation, a member of the Banff Forum and NEXUS communities, and a recipient of The Queen Elizabeth II Diamond Jubilee Medal.

Tina Roche
Community Foundation for Ireland (Lesson #36)

Tina was appointed CEO of The Foundation for Communities in January 2000. She established The Community Foundation for Ireland and Business in the Community Ireland and oversaw the development of Employment for People from Immigrant Communities, the Schools Business Partnership, The Linkage Programme (ex-offender placement) and Ready for Work encouraging business action on homelessness. Tina was Company Secretary of The Sunday Tribune and Head of Development from 1994 to 1999 for The National Gallery of Ireland. She served on the executive board of Amnesty International from 1992-1998; was a member of the Senate of the National University of Ireland from 1993-1997, and is a former board member of Volunteer Centres Ireland.

Gordon Thiessen
It Began with the Nominating Committee (Lesson #26)

After serving the Bank of Canada for 30 years in several senior positions, Gordon was appointed the sixth governor in 1994, for a term of seven years, retiring in 2001. He led Canada through seven of the most financially turbulent years in its history as governor. Believing Canadians should be better acquainted with the bank's business, he explained the complex workings of the world of finance to all manner of audiences—farmers, business associations and students alike. He received Honorary Doctor of Laws from the University of Saskatchewan and University of Ottawa and was made an Officer of the Order of Canada.

Jess Tomlin
"Think Big" (Lesson #7)

Jess Tomlin is the CEO of the Equality Fund. In this role, Jess leads an effort to resource feminist movements around the world working to change systems, shift power and dismantle barriers. She has worked in Sub-Saharan Africa, the Middle East, and Asia with organizations like the UN and World Bank. Prior to her role with the Equality Fund, she led the re-creation of the MATCH International Women's Fund, Canada's only global fund for women. Jess was named 2017's Most Innovative Woman of the Year by the Stevie Awards and received the Women of Influence award in 2020.

Margaret Torrance
You Don't Have to be a Millionaire to Make a Difference (Lesson #8)

Ken and Margaret first funded a McGill scholarship in honour of the Minister who married them, then endowed 5 scholarships at Carleton and 4 at their alma mater Guelph, plus Mentoring Awards at the National Arts Centre and GCTC. In 2015 they co-sponsored a Canadian composition of an Alice Munro's "Dear Life" inspired work which premiered at the National Arts Centre. Margaret is a Carleton alumna with a Master's degree from the School of Canadian and Indigenous Studies, and Ken, a Professor and Chair in Carleton's geography and environmental studies department until his passing in 2021.

Gillian Whyte
From Intern to Staff at OCF (Lesson #29)

- - - - -

Gillian joined the Community Foundation of Ottawa in 1998 as an Intern in Philanthropic Services and was the Senior Associate, Development and Donor Services when she left in 2011 to become the Senior Development Officer – Personal and Planned Giving at Carleton University. Gillian supports the Association of Gift Planners and their belief that leaving a deferred gift is a wonderful legacy. Gillian retired in 2020 after nine years at Carleton.

Photo: Justin Van Leeuwen

BARBARA MCINNES, C.M.
(1943-2021)

Barbara McInnes was with the Ottawa Community Foundation (OCF) since its inception in 1987. At the time of her retirement, OCF had grown into one of Canada's most highly respected and largest community foundations, with assets of $100 million and grant disbursements of over $6 million annually. Under her care, the Foundation engaged its local community in a number of leadership initiatives, creating a culture of collaborative philanthropy in the city and beyond.

Barbara was a founding Board member of Community Foundations of Canada and served on its Executive Committee for 13 years. She mentored six new Canadian Community Foundation CEOs during their first year on the job. She worked extensively with community foundations in North America and Europe, freely sharing her expertise and knowledge of organizational development and donor engagement.

Internationally, Barbara was a member of the Transatlantic Community Foundation Network for 13 years, dedicated to assisting the growth of community-based philanthropy in Europe and Mexico. She was also actively involved on a number of committees of the Council on Foundations in Washington, D.C., including the board's strategic planning committee.

Barbara was a frequent speaker locally, nationally and internationally on various philanthropic and community-based topics. She contributed a chapter to *Local Mission: Global Vision,* published in September 2008 by the Foundation Centre in New York, now available in four languages and wrote a paper "Growth

Cycles of Community Foundations" to present at the annual conference of the German Council on Foundations in Freiburg in 2004.

Other involvements
- Shorefast Foundation, Board Member and Chair of the Governance Committee
- Telus Friendly Future Foundation, Chair of the Ottawa Community Board
- PAL Ottawa, Advisory Committee
- Compassionate Ottawa, Advisory Board
- Refugee 613, Founding Board
- National Arts Centre Foundation, Governance and Nominating Committee
- Ottawa Philanthropy Awards, Co-Chair Selection Committee
- Impact Hub Ottawa, Board Member
- Women in Philanthropy Conference, Chair
- Ottawa Grantmakers' Forum, Chair
- The Learning Partnership, Ottawa Advisory Committee
- Ottawa Poverty Reduction Steering Committee, Co-Chair
- Transatlantic Community Foundation Network, Member
- Ottawa Estate Planning Council, President
- Carleton University, Board of Governors and Member of the Senate
- Leadership Ottawa and Ottawa Chamber of Voluntary Organizations, Co-founder
- Education Foundation of Ottawa, Honorary Advisory Board
- Peter F. Drucker Canadian Foundation for Innovation, Chair of the Selection Committee
- City of Ottawa's Arts Advisory Committee, Member
- Ottawa School of Art, Chair of the Board
- Margaret Atwood Gala, a fundraiser for the Ottawa Public Library, Chair
- United Way Ottawa, Board and Executive Committee member and Chair, Allocations and Agency Relations Committee.

Awards
- 2008 Order of Canada
- - - - -
- 2021 Lifetime Achievement Award, Association of Fundraising Professionals Ottawa Chapter
- 2016 Doctor of Laws, Honoris Causa, Carleton University
- 2014 Lifetime Achievement Award, Volunteer Ottawa
- 2012 Key to the City (presented to the Community Foundation)
- 2012 Recipient, Drew Shouldice Award, Ottawa Estate Planning Council
- 2010 Recipient, Quality of Life Award, St. Joe's Women's Centre
- 2009 Bronze Winner, Ottawa Chamber of Commerce Business Achievement Awards
- 2004 Community Service Award, Academy of Medicine Ottawa
- 2001 Volunteer of the Year, Volunteer Ottawa
- 1998 – 2009, various Wilmer Shields Rich Awards for communications
- 1998 Alastair Gamble Memorial Award for Excellence in Canadian Community Foundations
- 1997 Ottawa Philanthropy Award for Outstanding Fundraising Executive
- 1991 President's Award, United Way of Ottawa

Education
BA (Hons.) in Philosophy, Carleton University, Ottawa

Barbara lived most of her life in Ottawa, the community she loved and felt privileged to serve. From the age of 10 to 13, she and her family also lived in France where she developed lifelong friendships.

Married since 1963 to Glenn, they shared a deep interest in contemporary Canadian art and together, donated several hundred culturally significant pieces to: the Ottawa Art Gallery, Carleton University, the Beaverbrook Art Gallery, the National Gallery of Canada and Art Gallery of Alberta among others.

They are proud parents of two daughters, Leah Eustace and Emily McInnes and grandparents of Devon and Simon Eustace and Gideon Gallivan.

APPENDIX

LESSONS IN PHILANTHROPY— SUMMARY

1
We build community for the future and we don't do it alone.

2
Small grassroots organizations can have a lot of impact for a small amount of money.

3
Skillful management of one donor's generosity can lead to greater impact and a pipeline of support.

4
How you approach a situation will dictate how you come up with solutions and outcomes

5
Taking a leap of faith and supporting a "wild" idea can have long-term positive outcomes.

6
Having a forward-looking mindset sets the stage for collaboration, innovation and change.

7
Mission drives success.

8
Meeting donors where they are, will help to make their philanthropic dreams come true.

9
You can catalyze change by positively influencing those around you.

10
Determination and focus can co-exist with a gentle human touch.

11
Philanthropy is about providing people with an opportunity to invest in a good cause.

12
Engaging donors as "funders" can enrich the philanthropic experience for all.

13
Collaboration and consensus can be built with positive energy, clear communication and an open heart.

14
Keep an eye on the people and stories behind the numbers. Community service is about connection and relationships.

15
Find potential in others and then lift it up.

16
Lead with curiousity, passion and a bit of mischief.

17
Consider the impact that small charities can have on the community around them.

18
Respectfully challenging the status quo can lead to innovation and collaboration.

19
Sometimes having impact comes from connecting others with similar goals and objectives.

20
When possible, adopt a whole community approach.

21
Ideas, fueled by passion and accountability becomes a sustained vision for change.

22
Philanthropy intersects with community through the work of community foundations.

23
The grants program at the Ottawa Community Foundation led with trust and a transparent process of decision-making.

24
Lead by example.

25
Hard work today can have lasting impact into the future.

26
Excellent board members will lead to strong and effective board governance.

27
It's not difficult to manage money when everything's going well. A community foundation has a fiduciary responsibility to serve the community in good and bad times.

28
The rules of governance are critical to any
well-functioning organization.

29
Working directly with donors allowed the
Ottawa Community Foundation to quickly respond to
urgent grantee requests and community emergencies.

30
Doing the right thing in the moment, with a focus
on relationships, has an enduring effect.

31
Community foundations are about human capital;
working with people—donors and grantees—to find the
best possible way to invest in potential.

32
Act locally, think globally.

33
Modest beginnings can lead to great things.

34
Connect donors to projects.

35
Building authentic relationships will result in trust.

36
Start by listening.

APPENDIX

GROWING THE OTTAWA COMMUNITY FOUNDATION

Select Annual Report Excerpts, 1986 through 2013.

At the Community Foundation, every fund has a name, and every dollar has a story. Our annual reports provide us with an opportunity to tell some of these stories. They are examples of the great things that are happening in our community thanks to the generosity and vision of good people from every walk of life.—Barbara McInnes, 1995

Founding the Community Foundation of Ottawa–Carleton in 1986
When the Community Foundation's story began in 1986, Ottawa already had a wide variety of charitable and community organizations. Many people and groups were taking on different challenges facing the city and its citizens. Others were supporting activities that make the community a better place to live.

However, thirteen community leaders met on December 4, 1986, because they saw a gap. They believed that Ottawa needed an organization with a longer-term charitable orientation—a community foundation where donors would give money or other assets to be held in perpetuity.

The income generated by these assets will be put to work in the community, often to meet charitable priorities that might not have been anticipated at the time of the original donation. In other cases, donors designate broadly how the income is to be used—such as to meet the needs of children and young people or to support the arts.

The Meaning of a Million (1992)
In six years, the Community Foundation of Ottawa-Carleton has been able to help a steadily growing number of agencies and needs. Our grants now total more than $1 million.

In our first year, (1987) we were able to help 26 agencies with $36,685. In 1992, 100 agencies received grants, for a total of $310,000.

From a base of $500,000 in 1987, the Foundation's assets (including pledges and planned gifts) have grown to $7,904,794. To date there has been no administrative expenses charged against the funds. 100% of earnings have been given back to the community.

Hitting Milestones (1997)
We celebrated our 10th Anniversary with a sense of pride in what we have accomplished and with a sense of eagerness for the future.

Our permanent asset base grew to over $10 million and our expected future gifts of life insurance grew to over $20 million for a total of $30 million in planned gifts. More importantly we were able to take $850,000 in earnings from this asset base and reinvest it in 270 organizations who are making great things happen in our community.

Fifteen Years of Forever (2002)
We're standing at this milestone on our 15th Anniversary with vigour and optimism and pride. The balance sheet tells only part of the tale: assets of $66 million, grant distribution of $3.8 million. But as well, our vision of our role as a connector and a catalyst for the community, a center for philanthropy in fact, is taking form.

Our investment performance over our history has been outstanding. Although our return of 1.56% was significantly lower than in previous years, the Foundation's portfolio performed 6.3% above the benchmark and well above most community foundations in North America, for the third year in a row.

A Pivotal Year (2007)
We celebrated our twentieth birthday and now steward 600 funds entrusted to our care. The funds have grown in number and value, resulting in grant-making that has gone from a modest $33,000 in our first year, to an annual distribution to the community of about $6 million.

The economic climate in 2007 presented challenges to most investors and the Foundation was not immune to the volatility of the markets. From an investment return in 2006 of 12.4%, our portfolio generated a loss of $1.2 million in 2007. Prudently we developed a spending policy that allowed for the creation of reserves, which helped protect each fund. By drawing on these reserves, grant making continues in 2008 despite poor returns in 2007.

A Time for Celebration, Commemoration and Renewal (2012)
The Ottawa Community Foundation marked its first 25 years of forever. Together with the entire city we celebrated our accomplishments over the last quarter century; commemorated the many community leaders and volunteers who brought us to this point in our history; and worked together to renew our plans and commitments towards an ever more prosperous future. Investment returns of 9.4%, achieved in 2012, surpassing our benchmark of 8.0%, allowed us to provide close to $7 million in grants to 494 charitable organizations.

Barbara McInnes Announces Her Retirement after 26 years (2013)
Assets under management hit the $100 million mark. Investment returns of 15.3% were achieved after fees. $5.7 million was granted out to the community, bringing our total contribution over 26 years to almost $75 million.

> **In 2024, the Ottawa Community Foundation had assets of $281 million and granted $50 million to 872 charitable organizations.**

APPENDIX

GROWTH CYCLES OF COMMUNITY FOUNDATIONS

> *Presented by Barbara McInnes, President and CEO Community Foundation of Ottawa at the Annual Conference of the German Council on Foundations in Freiburg in 2004.*

This paper explores the growth of community foundations from infancy to maturity (and beyond). Some problems are normal, others are abnormal. It is important to know the difference so energies can be effectively focused. Board and staff of community foundations at every stage of development, by identifying the issues their foundation will face over the course of its life cycle, will be better prepared to deal with the present and plan for the future.

When one considers all of the complicating matters—community type and size, community make-up, and foundation history—it becomes clear that any combination of factors can accelerate or impede the growth and development of any given community foundation. What we want to concentrate on here are not the differences but the similarities.

The objective is to describe a typical life cycle for a community foundation regardless of other influences and complications. In doing so, I hope to help staff and board members:

- anticipate and prepare for the challenges related to each new phase;
- determine the best style of leadership for each stage; and

- help foundations that may be low-performing or "stuck" at a particular stage of growth understand the reasons and take steps to improve their chances of future success.

There are innumerable models that can be used to describe organizational life cycles and management styles. For purposes of simplicity and consistency, I have chosen that of Dr. Ichak Adizes. This paper adapts his corporate lifecycle framework to the work of community foundations.

The Organizational Lifecycle

In discussing organizational lifecycles it's important to remember that the phases do not correspond to chronological age or to asset size. These are not the determining factors of placement on the lifecycle chart. So, as I describe the stages, consider where your foundation may be, based on the particular set of characteristics typical of that stage.

At each stage of growth, there are opportunities for the organization to regress or move forward. Particular internal or external circumstances can cause your foundation to move through stages faster or slower. Usually, significant events occur in each stage that are necessary to move forward in a foundation's development. You are in the best position to determine at which stage your particular community foundation currently "fits."

At every stage on the growth side of the lifecycle, there are normal problems faced by organizations. These are simply the natural challenges of growing up, appropriate to each stage of development. Human infants cannot walk immediately after birth but that is a normal problem. An adolescent who loses the ability to walk would get rushed to hospital. That would be an extremely abnormal problem for an able-bodied individual at that point in their development.

If you have a lot of problems, that's a good sign. It means you're changing. When you have no problems, you're probably dead. If there is no change, mediocrity eventually catches up. Change is positive for good performers and very bad for poor performers. Having problems is a good sign—if you know what to do about it. Problems that are not treated at the right time are crises in waiting.

The following graphic depicts the organizational lifecycle I am going to describe.

The jagged marks show particularly difficult transitions. The letters PAEI relate to different management styles, which are more fully described in a later section.

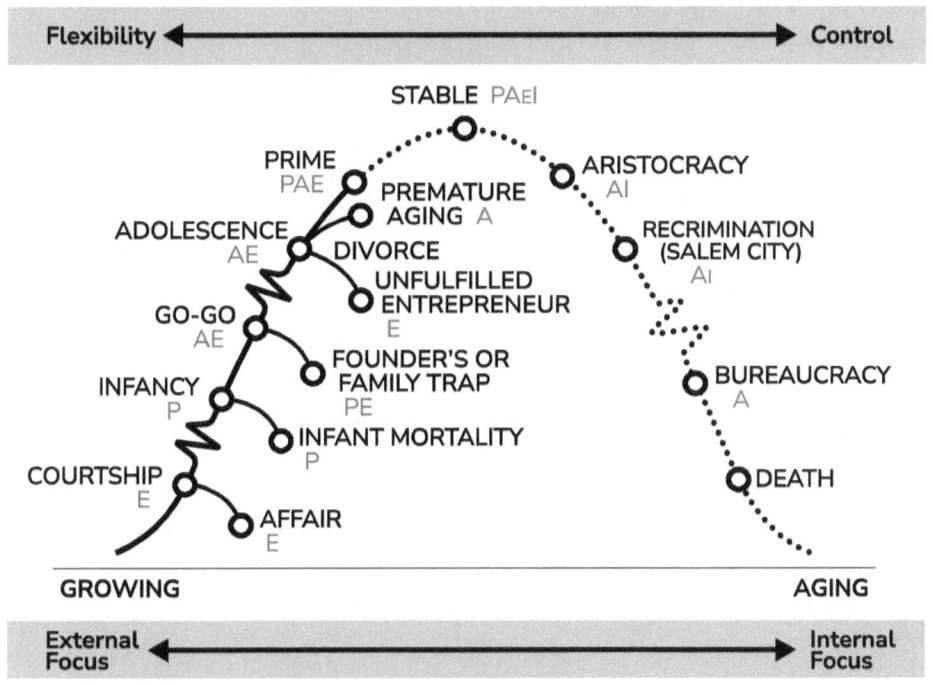

All graphics and charts of the Adizes Methodology courtesy of Management Vitality.

When you drive in a foreign city you drive slower. When you know the road ahead, you can go much faster. Usually, in a fast-changing organization, marketing and development change in response to a changing environment. Accounting and finance lag behind.

The trick is to not grow all at once. The only logical other progression is down. It's just a question of time. Think about adding to a building. If the original design is for three floors and demand is growing, you don't just add the 4th, 5th and 6th floors. The building will collapse if you don't first reinforce the foundation. An organization can outgrow its infrastructure very quickly—it's like buying trousers for a growing child.

Lifecycle Phases

a) Courtship

Courtship is the stage at which all new life begins. People get together and conceive of a new organization and build a vision. It's a very exciting time. This is the vision or idea stage, where the community foundation has not yet formalized. Imagination and inspiration abound. The primary question is whether the dream for this foundation can be realized. This stage is characterized by enthusiasm, energy and creativity, usually driven by two or three people including one charismatic leader.

At this stage, initiators are busy getting others to share in their enthusiasm and commitment. It is essential that they engage the right people. Who these people are will vary widely from community to community. Whatever other characteristics they may have, they need to have one thing in common—they should be the community's "influencers" i.e. the people who have the most influence to shape opinion and not necessarily in formal ways. A common mistake is to think that a lot of wealthy people need to be on-side in these early days. What is more important than wealth is that the founders attract people who have the community's respect and who can, in turn, influence those with wealth.

Characteristics—Normal problems and natural challenges
- Idealistic vision
- Excitement and enthusiasm
- A great deal of time is devoted to building commitment to the vision
- Strong, charismatic founder clearly in control
- Leadership comes from volunteers
- Frequent meetings
- Very few resources
- Long-term funding not in place and even requirements are not clear

Abnormal problems that threaten viability of the organization
- Fear and doubt
- Rigid policies and procedures in place
- Few meetings
- Lack of commitment
- Lack of interest in other ideas
- Inflexible or unrealistic long-term financial plan

- No interest in learning
- Unrealistic fanatical founder
- Leaders unable to inspire commitment from others

b) Infancy

This is the start-up phase of the foundation, when it incorporates, creates its bylaws, receives its official status as a charity and recruits its first board.

High energy and creativity continue, with a more focused imperative on how to raise the funding needed. An office is established and the first printed materials developed.

Infant organizations require constant, 24-hour care from their founders. There are always near-disasters to clean up and constant feedings are required. Just as human infants cry for milk, infant community foundations cry for "money! money! money!"

Characteristics—Normal problems and natural challenges
- Leadership is a one-person show but is willing to listen
- No managerial depth
- Little delegation
- Hard work and risk-taking nourish the commitment
- Few policies, procedures, budgets and systems
- Try everything, take risks, make mistakes
- Support system (personal and external) encouraging and supportive
- Need for financial resources focuses all activity
- Urgent need for operating funds, "We don't need any more ideas, we need money"

Abnormal problems that threaten viability of the organization
- Prolonged extreme demands erode commitment, lead to burn-out
- Chronic negative cash flow
- Focus on managing rather than doing the work
- Premature delegation
- Founder is arrogant
- Founder's views are ignored
- Aversion to risk; no tolerance for mistakes
- Loss of personal and external support systems causes founder to turn away from the organization

- Need for money is not recognized, board unwilling or unable to see this as priority

c) Go-Go

The Go-Go stage is the toddler stage. An organization gets its first attractive opportunities and frantically scrambles to get results. Sometimes at this stage an "angel investor" emerges, providing financial support while the infant learns to stand on its own.

The organization wants to get into everything and touches anything that crosses its path, just like human toddlers. Foundations get involved in a wide variety of activity, accept all kinds of gifts and try everything that comes their way.

Characteristics—Normal problems and natural challenges
- See endless opportunities, think they can do everything
- The organization chart (if it exists) is messy, constantly changing, organized around people, not functions.
- Leader is a "happy juggler", everyone does everything
- Leadership is centralized; tasks are delegated but not responsibility
- Board takes direction from and supports the leader
- Commitment grows; there are now many stakeholders
- Too many priorities, highly flexible focus
- Tendency to equate asset growth with success
- First paid staff
- Office space is no or low cost, loaned or shared

Abnormal problems that threaten viability of the organization
- Arrogance and the temptation to try everything is unmitigated by acknowledgement of risks
- Clearly defined organization chart and position descriptions
- People are inflexible or burnt out
- No decision-making outside the leader or core group
- Board exerts control, diverges from leader
- Commitment stagnates, remains with an internal group
- Clearly defined priorities lack flexibility
- No one takes responsibility for building the assets
- Continue to operate with volunteers in order to save money
- Operate from a board member's basement

d) Adolescence

Adolescence is a difficult time. Organizations have to figure out who they are, what their purpose and their role in the world must be. They have to come to terms with limitations, and make difficult choices to forgo some opportunities and focus their energies. It's a time fraught with danger for organizations.

The overriding question is how to build the community foundation to be viable. Serious questions are raised about the business of the foundation and its financial sustainability. Accountability becomes important. Controls and organizational systems are needed but may be resisted.

Characteristics—Normal problems and natural challenges
- Few founders left on the board
- Board exercises new control over management
- Board in transition between working, hands-on model and governance, policy model
- Board and staff roles fuzzy; frequently step on each other's toes
- Administration and bureaucracy gain importance
- Conflict between entrepreneurial leader and administrators
- Yo-yo delegation
- Policies developed but not followed
- Lots of committees
- Too many meetings

Abnormal problems that threaten viability of the organization
- Revert to Go-Go
- Founder's trap
- Board loses confidence in staff leadership
- Infighting
- CEO toppling
- Entrepreneur replaced by administrator; bureaucracy takes over
- Paralysis due to power shifting back and forth
- "Us" vs. "them" cliques and factions
- Inconsistent organizational goals
- Rapid decline in mutual respect

e) Prime

Organizations that survive Adolescence by growing up, without growing old, enter an optimal state called Prime. At Prime, an organization is systematic enough to replicate success and nimble and adaptive enough to evolve—solving problems caused by change and staying young and vital. This is the maturing stage for the community foundation when it is experiencing steady growth.

The questions now become:

- how to continue the momentum
- how to maintain stability without growing stale or losing creativity and enthusiasm
- how to make the best use of finite resources.

The organization achieves a reasonable comfort level in operations. Fees and endowment are generating adequate income and enabling higher levels of professional staffing. Administrative systems are in place and long-range planning are undertaken. Often the first bequests are realized. The investment portfolio is diversified and financial issues are more complex.

The foundation is known and appreciated in the community. This stage sometimes coincides with a change in leadership at both the board and staff levels.

Characteristics—Normal problems and natural challenges
- Board has fewer meetings; concentrates on oversight of management, policy development and long-range planning
- Board vs staff roles defined and respected
- Professional, more specialized staff in place with responsibilities clearly defined and appropriately delegated
- Management team contains a balance of styles
- Major focus on human resources; chronic shortage of good people
- The community looks to the foundation for leadership
- Not enough discretionary money available; need unrestricted funds
- Conflict between priorities: asset growth, serving the community, internal administration
- Technology is important, imposing demand for expertise and resources
- New opportunities explored; not all are successful; there is tolerance for moderate risk

- Balanced self-control & flexibility
- Predictable performance

Abnormal problems that threaten the viability of the organization
- Rely on past successes
- Structure departments or divisions around people vs. functions
- Move to a "we used to do that" mode
- Become smug; stop striving; lose the "edge"
- Focus in, instead of out

f) Stable

Something terrible happens when the main focus of the community foundation at its Prime turns inwards. If more attention is paid to the internal than the external environment, the foundation can fall out of step with the times. Having recently been at Prime, foundations can get cocky and begin acting as if they can dictate what needs to happen in the external environment. Although they do not realize it, their vitality has been sapped, flexibility impaired and rigidity begins to set in.

Abnormal problems that threaten the viability of the organization
- Losing flexibility
- More time spent on internal issues than external
- New ideas unwelcome, no longer exciting
- Finance and administration are more important than asset development, grantmaking and community convening
- Expectations lowered for asset growth
- Focus on past achievements
- Paralysis—unable to deal with uncertainties of the future

g) Aristocracy

The community foundation has turned so far inward that it feels like an exclusive club. The internal hierarchy of office politics supports a self-congratulatory elite. Internal matters have become more important than the "customers" (i.e. donors and the community). The customers may even be seen as a nuisance, diverting attention away from the very important internal matters people in Aristocratic foundations busy themselves with. This leads to real decline for the organization, but few acknowledge it yet. Those who crave a more vital, renewed organization quietly begin to leave.

Abnormal problems that threaten the viability of the organization
- Emphasis on how, rather than what or why
- "Don't make waves" attitude
- Growth slows (except bequests)
- Donors and community find it hard to be heard
- Board is elitist, a group of cronies, little new blood
- CEO more involved in national initiatives, pays little attention to local
- Ongoing operating surpluses
- Bequests give appearance of sustainable growth
- Need to re-invent and re-energize the organization
- Excitement is absent

h) Salem City

After a while, the foundation's reversal of fortune becomes impossible to ignore. The smug, incestuous politics of the once Aristocratic organization turns nasty. Salem City is characterized by witch-hunts. Scapegoats are eagerly sought. Blame is flung from one person to another like a hot potato. There are mutinies and defections. This is the last chance for the foundation to pull out of its nosedive, pay attention to its overall situation, and rebuild itself back towards Prime.

Abnormal problems that threaten the viability of the organization
- Emphasis on who caused the problem rather than on solving it
- Backstabbing and infighting
- Focus on internal turf wars
- External customer becomes a nuisance
- Non-alignment with its primary markets

i) Bureaucracy

If the witch-hunts of Salem City rage on to their bitter conclusion, all potential movers and shakers get driven out of the organization. The people who are left try to normalize things by building up processes and procedures to bring the organization back under control. However, the focus remains on the internal workings of the foundation, not on its mission and values. Policies breed more policies and the organization degenerates into Bureaucracy. Return to Prime at this late stage becomes extremely difficult if not impossible.

Abnormal problems that threaten the viability of the organization
- Many systems but little functionality
- Internal focus
- Lots of policies without real control

j) Death

The final curtain awaits all organizations that carry on after they have lost their vision, mission and values. If the only thing keeping a community foundation going is the historic endowed assets, it will become irrelevant and ultimately collapse—though this may take much longer than organizations that are not built on endowments.

Abnormal problems that threaten the viability of the organization
- No real commitment but people will go to great lengths to preserve their jobs
- Death may take years while the foundation is in a vegetative state on the artificial life support of its endowments
- There is learned helplessness, an "if only" mentality

Management Styles

Adizes describes four categories, which can be spoken of as "management styles," although the underlying concepts are generic and can apply to more than just management. They are the "PAEI" first referred to on page 137. Most people naturally blend a few of these styles, and many of us develop skills in all four. However, no one is equally strong in each area over the long-term. Everyone has at least one dominant style and often a secondary style which is almost as natural as the first. When leaders are engaged in managing organizational growth, they quickly learn that people react to change differently. They define problems differently and prefer different kinds of solutions.

The Producer (P)

The Producer has the drive and discipline necessary to see real results produced. Goal-oriented, impatient, active, and always busy, the Producer has little time for idle chitchat. Direct and to the point, typical Producers are behind-the-scenes movers and shakers. Many Producers are attracted to high-intensity departments such as Sales. They are too busy to waste time with meetings. They prefer to cut the small talk and get out there to get the job done.

The Administrator (A)
The Administrator ensures that rules are in place and followed, that plans are made and adhered to. Precise and accurate, the Administrator creates methods and procedures to make sure things are done right. Systematic, analytical and logical, Administrators clean up other people's carelessness. They like to keep the organization humming at a steady pace and are willing to do things more slowly and carefully, making certain that procedures are followed properly. Administrators are drawn to tasks that require systemic thinking and precision, such as accounting.

The Entrepreneur (E)
The Entrepreneur is an idea person, always asking "why?" or "why not?" A visionary with dreams, plans and schemes, the Entrepreneur leads others to ideas that they would not pursue on their own. Success for an Entrepreneur requires both creativity and risk. They sometimes get bored with short-term tasks, and prefer developing the long-term vision. Entrepreneurs are charismatic, and often generate ideas for new projects, new approaches to problems, or even new businesses.

The Integrator (I)
The Integrator is people-oriented. True Integrators value social harmony, and thrive on peacemaking and teamwork. An organizer of social events, the Integrator's pleasantness is unmistakable. Amiable and empathetic, the Integrator is the first to cooperate in helping with tasks or problems. Integrators make the workplace feel friendly. They prefer to work by consensus, instead of taking a strong position against others. Integrators are attracted to people-oriented occupations like human resource development. (**Please note that personnel administration, which usually falls under human resources is an A(dministrator) style job, not an I(ntegrator) style job. It is training or development that is I.

When making a decision, all of these perspectives need to be brought to the table. Not surprising then that the inevitable consequence is conflict. However, this does not have to mean factions and bad feelings. In a setting of mutual trust and respect, all parties realize that the best solutions are derived from a full consideration of all perspectives. If the foundation's mission, values and goals are forefront, it becomes okay to question ideas and challenge decisions. When different perspectives are valued, conflict actually strengthens the organization.

Refer back to the chart on page 137 which illustrates the styles that are best suited to particular lifecycle stages. PAE and I styles are constantly at odds with each other so when problems arise, each views the issues from a different perspective. No individual can equally embrace all the styles but teams and organizations can. By bringing together complementary teams of people with different strengths, organizations can cover all the bases. The challenge is not to avoid conflict but to constructively manage natural conflicts between these four perspectives.

Take a few moments to reflect on your own particular management style and the styles of others in your organization.

- Are you too heavily weighted toward one leadership type?
- Where do you need balance, based upon your particular stage of growth?

This sort of analysis can be helpful in determining the qualities of new hires as you grow your organization.

The Quest for Prime
According to many community foundation authorities, an ideal environment for a community foundation today would be a large enough region (say 250,000 to 500,000 population) with a thriving urban center where most decision-makers can be identified and reached.

The region should be suitably diverse, including a university and hospital, and its economy supported by a healthy mix of industry and white-collar professions. The population base should go back many generations with the tradition of philanthropy well-established.

The ideal community foundation will have excellent representation from the region's most respected leaders on its board. Those leaders will have set aside or guaranteed adequate resources to cover the operating expenses until it has accumulated sufficient endowment or other financial resources for self-sufficiency. They will have invested in competent, full-time staffing for the foundation and they will play an active role as ambassadors, introducing foundation staff to all those who should know of it within their region.

As it grows, the ideal community foundation will develop a strong, respected institutional presence in its region, based upon the quality of leadership it has shown. It will have mutually supportive relationships with the region's top nonprofit organizations and private foundations, and (in North America) excellent relations with the top estate planning professionals.

The board leadership of this foundation will be a model of governance, excel in strategic planning, community convening, grantmaking and investment management. There will be a significant focus on human resources through constant training and retreats for both board and staff members. Succession plans will be in place for senior staff and board members.

The community foundation staff will be sized appropriately for its budget, and will reflect the various types of leadership skills needed for a well-rounded organization.

Chances are, while any given community foundation environment will have many of these characteristics, it will not have them all. Various benchmarks have been developed over the years but there are no useful rules linking such things as assets or grantmaking activity to staff levels or board size.

Many comparisons have been done but, not surprisingly, they fail to show definitively how to go about ensuring that a given community foundation achieves and maintains its Prime. Just as we know that parenting books cannot tell us how to raise perfect adults, we can nevertheless acknowledge the usefulness of the guidance they provide.

The greatest threats to a mature foundation's ability to stay in Prime:
1. Complacency Staff, board become bored, passive. The foundation is no longer be seen as a vibrant player in its community. New asset growth from living donors slows, though growth through bequests may give the impression of a healthy organization for many more years. The board loses members. Programs become repetitive, stale. Large staff turnover occurs.

2. Arrogance Staff becomes remote, elitist. The reputation of the foundation begins to suffer. The board is less involved in making decisions. Very few are involved in making grants. The foundation is seen as hard to reach, serving a small constituency with narrow interests. Outreach is minimal.

3. Community Gadfly Senior staff and board become concerned with their image as part of the establishment, and community insiders. They belong to the best clubs, serve on commissions, give and receive awards, attend all of the right events, are quoted in the media. Older donors begin to feel slighted and forgotten. The marginalized community feels irrelevant. New fund growth slows. Operational funds spent for perks increase.

4. CEO Toppling Sudden, unplanned change at the top of the organization can be one of the worst things to happen to any community foundation. Almost always, it will cause the organization to lose momentum and revert to an earlier stage of its life cycle. If the CEO embodied the foundation's entrepreneurial, creative aspect, bureaucracy will take over and growth will stop. Key stakeholders will become disenchanted and mistrustful. The situation can result from destructive conflict between the E and A styles, with A doing an end run around the CEO, directly to the Board. The Board members must be vigilant in order not to get drawn in.

5. Mission Drift Sometimes community foundations run into trouble when they allow their primary mission to be overtaken by another agenda, perhaps brought to the table by an aggressive director, donor or politician. This could include running charitable programs, focusing too many resources on a single set of issues, or simply carrying out the philanthropic agenda of a major donor.

Conclusion
Among the useful lessons learned by studying the community foundation life cycle:

- Some problems at each stage are normal; others are abnormal.
- Teamwork involving mutual trust and respect is vital to success.
- Different leadership styles can be adversarial or complementary, depending how they are managed.
- Different combinations of leadership styles are required at different stages in the lifecycle.
- Prime is not a destination. It's a condition. The organization is still growing, therefore not at the top of the curve.

Acknowledgement: The work of Mike Rawl, CEO of the Mid-Shore Community Foundation, was the inspiration for this paper.

Reference: Adizes, I. Managing Corporate Lifecycles, Prentice Hall Press, 1999

We care about your opinion of
Lessons in Philanthropy: The Legacy of Barb McInnes.

Your feedback will help us share this book with others in non-profits, foundations, and community organizations. Please take a moment to complete this short survey.

www.BarbarasLegacy.ca/reader-survey

Barbara McInnes Legacy Fund

We encourage you to make a $20 donation to the Barbara McInnes Legacy Fund at the Ottawa Community Foundation for each book you order. A Canadian tax receipt will be issued.

www.ocf-fco.ca/barbara-mcinnes-legacy-fund

Barbara McInnes worked tirelessly to enhance philanthropy for almost four decades. Her warmth, wisdom, and generosity inspired countless professionals. This fund is a way to carry forward her spirit—by fostering mentorship, sharing knowledge, and building a stronger philanthropic community in her memory.

Order The Book

www.ingramcontent.com/pod-product-compliance
Lightning Source LLC
Chambersburg PA
CBHW032040290426
44110CB00012B/885